antojitos

antojitos

FESTIVE AND FLAVORFUL MEXICAN SMALL PLATES

BARBARA SIBLEY & MARGARITTE MALFY

with Mary Goodbody

Photography by Lucy Schaeffer

TEN SPEED PRESS

BERKELEY

37

EL MUNDO

Published in the United States by Ten Speed Press, an
imprint of the Crown Publishing Group, a division of
Random House, Inc., New York.
www.crownpublishing.com
www.tenspeed.com

Ten Speed Press and the Ten Speed Press colophon are
registered trademarks of Random House, Inc.

Images on pages iv, vii, 20, 30, 38, 42, 55, 58,
80, 102, 123, 125, and 128 © Ediciones Malinalco.
www.edicionesmalinalco.com

Library of Congress Cataloging-in-Publication Data
on file with publisher

ISBN 978-1-58008-929-6

Printed in China

Design by Katy Brown

10 9 8 7 6 5 4 3 2

First Edition

CONTENTS

INTRODUCTION

AS ANYONE WHO LIKES TO COOK CAN UNDERSTAND, when we sat down to write this cookbook, our first, we wanted to pack the pages with every recipe and bit of food lore we know as a way of sharing our passion for Mexican food and culture. But we quickly realized we had to rein in our eagerness—if not our enthusiasm—when choosing dishes to include. We finally decided to focus on the small bites, or *antojitos*, that Mexicans have been serving for centuries.

At La Palapa, our two restaurants in Manhattan, our guests share our delight in genuine Mexican food and especially enjoy our *antojitos*. But it wasn't until our fifth-anniversary fiesta that we realized that the most celebratory way to share our flavorful food was to create a savory meal composed solely of *antojitos*. We furiously cooked *chalupas*, quesadillas, *taquitos*, and more, and couldn't get the platters out of the kitchen fast enough! Our guests raved about these small treasures, which helped set this book in motion.

In Mexico, *antojitos* are sometimes eaten as appetizers before a meal, as they often are at La Palapa, but they are usually sold in small stalls in marketplaces or town plazas. Visit any outdoor Mexican market and you will immediately detect their heady aromas wafting through the air. Your senses will compete joyfully with one another—sight, hearing, smell, and touch—and beckon you to satisfy your fifth sense: taste. The word *antojo* means "craving," which explains the name of these tasty, fresh bites.

In some parts of Mexico, an *antojito* is called a *tentempie*, roughly, "a snack that keeps you standing"—in other words, a bite to tide you over until your next meal. These snacks are typically eaten out of hand or from a small paper cone or cup while standing or walking around. Although *antojitos* are not usually considered a full meal by Mexicans, they can be so bountiful and delectable that there is no reason not to add a margarita or a beer and declare an assortment of them a suitable supper.

Every region in Mexico boasts its typical *antojitos*. Sometimes the same name is found in more than one region, although it refers to different foods. The opposite is also true. You may find that the *antojito* you sampled in Chiapas is called something quite different in Oaxaca or the Yucatán. No worries. Whatever they are called, they are invariably satisfying, and their long history, from the days of the Aztec markets to today's plaza stalls, has ensured that each generation has added its own *sazón*, or "seasoning," by introducing a new salsa or a new filling or a new garnish.

Perhaps what we like best about *antojitos*—beyond their sheer deliciousness—is that several served at one time can transform any gathering into a festive occasion. If you are planning a party, they are ideal. When we cater parties from our restaurant kitchen, we generally offer six or seven *antojitos*. But for a party at home, three or four will do. We have put together five fiesta menus for this book to demonstrate how to mix and match our *antojitos* for a party. Follow our suggestions and then go with your own ideas. You can't go wrong.

La Palapa is not your everyday Mexican restaurant. When you are seated in our Manhattan restaurants, your experience is far closer to dining in Mexico City than to eating in most "Mexican" restaurants in the United States. We pride ourselves on serving true Mexican food in all its complexity. Our recipes derive from Mexican home cooking, rather than restaurant cooking, and every dish is made with fresh, natural, authentic ingredients. Indeed, we are happiest when our guests from Mexico tell us our food "tastes like home."

Our recipes are traditional and artisanal, collected over many years of travel and living in Mexico. Our *mole negro oaxaqueño* (black mole from Oaxaca) calls for more than two dozen ingredients, and our *salsas de mesa* (table salsas) are carefully assembled with seasonal ingredients from Mexico. Purslane, nopal cactus, and *huitlacoche* inspire us, turning up in salads, tamales, and delicate crêpes, respectively. Even something typically as prosaic as *totopos* (tortilla chips) is special at La Palapa, where we make them from blue, yellow, and white tortillas and season them with cumin and sea salt. We have included recipes for these restaurant favorites and more in this book.

Since opening La Palapa, we have traveled together extensively throughout Mexico, and with every trip we have expanded our knowledge of the country's cooking. With this book on *antojitos*, we hope to pass along some of what we have learned about this complex and endlessly intriguing cuisine.

1

bebidas y botanas
COCKTAILS AND SNACKS

margarita clásica de la palapa
**LA PALAPA'S FRESH
LIME MARGARITA** / 2

zihua margarita
ZIHUA MARGARITA / 3

margarita de flor de jamaica
HIBISCUS MARGARITA / 4

agua fresca de jamaica
HIBISCUS WATER / 4

paloma de mango y mezcal
**MANGO-MEZCAL
PALOMA** / 6

sangría blanca con jamaica
**WHITE HIBISCUS
SANGRIA** / 7

tequila y sangrita
**TEQUILA WITH
SANGRITA** / 9

sangría roja de citricos
RED CITRUS SANGRIA / 9

mojito de tequila y sandía
**WATERMELON AND
TEQUILA MOJITO** / 10

michelada
**SPICY MEXICAN BEER
COCKTAIL** / 11

chelada
**MEXICAN BEER
COCKTAIL** / 11

agua fresca de tamarindo
TAMARIND WATER / 12

guacamole de la palapa
**LA PALAPA'S CLASSIC
GUACAMOLE** / 14

guacamole con tomatillo y durazno
**GUACAMOLE WITH
TOMATILLO AND
PEACH** / 15

totopos de la palapa
**LA PALAPA'S TORTILLA
CHIPS** / 15

tostadas traditionales
**TRADITIONAL
TOSTADAS** / 16

quesadillas de tres quesos
**THREE-CHEESE
QUESADILLAS** / 17

aceitunas sazonadas
SEASONED OLIVES / 18

cacahuates enchilados
**SPICY ROASTED
PEANUTS** / 18

SEVERAL TALES EXIST on the origin of the margarita, all of them dating to the 1940s. We like the story of Santos Cruz, a bartender in Galveston, Texas, who allegedly created the margarita for singer Peggy Lee, with the help of Margaret Sames, another Texan, who rimmed Miss Lee's glass with salt. But the most credible account names Carlos "Danny" Herrara, owner of Rancho La Gloria restaurant in Tijuana, Mexico, who invented the drink for American actress Marjorie King. Herrara knew that King was allergic to all liquors except tequila, so he concocted a tequila and citrus cocktail and named it in her honor.

la palapa's fresh lime margarita

MARGARITA CLÁSICA DE LA PALAPA

SERVES 1

1½ slices lime
Kosher salt
Ice cubes
2 ounces (¼ cup) Sour Mix (page 138)
2½ ounces (5 tablespoons) blanco tequila
Scant 1 ounce (2 tablespoons) orange-flavored liqueur, such as triple sec or Cointreau
½ ounce (1 tablespoon) freshly squeezed orange juice

Rub the rim of the glass with the whole lime slice. Use a 12-ounce glass for a margarita on the rocks; use a martini glass for a margarita straight up. Spread the salt on a small plate large enough for the rim of the glass, and dip the rim into the salt to coat. Set the glass aside.

Fill a cocktail shaker or small pitcher with ice cubes. Add the sour mix, tequila, liqueur, and orange juice. Shake about 5 times, or until frothy and nicely chilled. Or, if using a pitcher, stir well with a long-handled wooden spoon.

Fill the glass with ice cubes if serving on the rocks. Strain the margarita into the prepared glass. Slit the remaining ½ lime slice partway, balance the slice on the glass rim, and serve.

FOR US, THE LOVELY SEASIDE TOWN of Zihuatanejo on Mexico's Pacific coast is paradise. We first tried this smoky, tart margarita on a flower-filled terrace near the town's pretty Playa La Ropa, with its soft sand and blue water. A splash of *mezcal* provides the smokiness, which blends with the light oak flavor of the *reposado* tequila.

Back in New York, we made the margarita with Mezcal de Rancho, literally "*mezcal* from the ranch," a high-proof home-distilled *agave espadín*. We now use Del Maguey brand Chichicapa *mezcal*, which is produced in a single village and conjures up the home-brewed flavor of the original. This margarita is best served straight up in a glass rimmed with salt.

zihua margarita

ZIHUA MARGARITA

SERVES 1

1½ slices lime

About 2 tablespoons kosher salt

Ice cubes

2 ounces (¼ cup) Sour Mix (page 138)

2 ounces (¼ cup) reposado tequila, such as Sauza Hornitos brand

Scant 1 ounce (2 tablespoons) orange-flavored liqueur, such as Cointreau, triple sec, or Patrón Citrónge

½ ounce (1 tablespoon) freshly squeezed orange juice

½ ounce (1 tablespoon) mezcal, such as Del Maguey Chichicapa brand

Rub the rim of a martini glass with the whole lime slice. Spread the salt on a small plate large enough for the rim of the glass, and dip the rim into the salt to coat.

Fill a cocktail shaker or small pitcher with ice cubes. Add the sour mix, tequila, liqueur, orange juice, and *mezcal*. Shake about 5 times, or until frothy and nicely chilled. Or, if using a pitcher, stir well with a long-handled wooden spoon.

Strain the margarita into the prepared glass. Slit the remaining ½ lime slice partway, balance the slice on the glass rim, and serve.

THIS HIBISCUS MARGARITA, a house specialty, includes a little *piquín* chile–laced salt for color and fire. Like so many inspirations, adding the spiced salt, which we previously used only for one of our beer cocktails (page 11), came about by accident. One hot summer day, Margaritte decided to rim the margarita glasses with it, and everyone liked it. Now, we use the spiced salt for many of our margaritas.

hibiscus margarita
MARGARITA DE FLOR DE JAMAICA

SERVES 4

1 lime, quartered
Piquín Chile Salt (page 138)
Ice cubes
8 ounces (1 cup) blanco tequila
6 ounces (¾ cup) Sour Mix (page 138)
2 ounces (¼ cup) Hibiscus Water (this page)
4 ounces (½ cup) orange-flavored liqueur, such as triple sec or Cointreau
Splash of freshly squeezed orange juice
2 lime slices, halved

Rub the rim of each glass with a lime quarter. Use 12-ounce glasses for margaritas on the rocks; use martini glasses for margaritas straight up. Spread the chile salt on a small plate large enough for the rim of a glass, and dip each rim into the salt to coat. Set the glasses aside.

Fill a pitcher with ice. Add the tequila, sour mix, Hibiscus Water, liqueur, and a splash of orange juice. Stir well until frothy and nicely chilled.

Fill the glasses with ice cubes if serving on the rocks. Strain the margaritas into the prepared glasses, garnish with lime, and serve.

WE SERVE THIS hibiscus-flavored *agua fresca* on its own and use it as an ingredient in our cocktails.

hibiscus water
AGUA FRESCA DE JAMAICA

MAKES ABOUT 8 CUPS; SERVES 6

½ cup dried hibiscus flowers (see Cook's Note)
8 cups water
About ½ cup sugar

In a 2-quart nonreactive saucepan, boil the flowers in the water for 10 minutes, or until they lose some of their color and are reconstituted and plump.

Pour the contents of the pan through a sieve set over a pitcher or bowl. Discard the contents of the sieve. Sweeten the deep red liquid with the sugar, stirring until the sugar dissolves. Hibiscus is very tart!

Allow to cool completely, then taste again and adjust for sweetness. Transfer to a large jar with a tight-fitting lid. It will keep in the refrigerator for up to 5 days.

To serve, pour over ice in tall glasses.

COOK'S NOTE: *Dried hibiscus flowers are available in specialty stores that feature dried flowers, herbs, and other aromatics, or on the Internet at www.mexgrocer.com and other sites selling Mexican ingredients.*

LA PALOMA—"The Dove"—is the name of a popular cocktail in Mexico City. Squirt, a local grapefruit soda, and tequila are poured over ice in a salt-rimmed glass. Here, it is taken up a notch with the addition of *mezcal* and mango puree. At La Palapa, we use a Mexican grapefruit soda called Jarritos, although any grapefruit soda, such as Fizzy Lizzy, or even grapefruit juice can be used. We also serve a shot glass of *reposado* tequila alongside.

mango-mezcal paloma
PALOMA DE MANGO Y MEZCAL

SERVES 1

1½ slices lime
Piquín Chile Salt (page 138)
Ice cubes
2 ounces (¼ cup) tequila
1½ ounces (3 tablespoons) mezcal
1 ounce (2 tablespoons) mango puree
    (see Cook's Note)
1 teaspoon chopped fresh cilantro
    leaves (optional)
1 (13½-ounce) bottle grapefruit soda

Rub the rim of a tall glass with the whole lime slice. Spread the chile salt on a small plate large enough for the rim of the glass, and dip the rim into the salt to coat.

Fill the glass with ice cubes. Add the tequila, *mezcal*, mango puree, and cilantro, if using, to the glass and stir to mix the cilantro with the liquid. Slowly add about one-third of the soda.

Slit the remaining ½ lime slice partway and balance the slice on the glass rim. Serve at once, with the remaining soda on the side.

COOK'S NOTE: *Thaw frozen mango puree, or puree a ripe mango in a blender to make your own.*

MEZCAL

The name *mezcal* is given to all spirits made from the juice of the *piña* (heart of the agave), which is cooked, fermented, and then distilled. This means that tequila is technically *mezcal:* both are made from agave, though *mezcal* can be made from more than two dozen different varieties and tequila is made only from the blue variety grown in designated areas. They are both distilled, as well. But *mezcal* is ready to drink after a single distillation, and tequila requires at least two distillations and then careful filtering to mellow its taste.

Mezcal typically has a more concentrated color and a more potent flavor than tequila, and it often has a smoky taste, considered a desirable trait, because the agave is baked in an underground kiln. Tequila and *mezcal* also part ways when it comes to the maguey worm, which some Oaxacan *mezcal* producers include in their bottles. They maintain that because the worm feeds on the agave plant, it contains a concentrated essence of the plant that enhances the flavor of the liquor. Worms are sought and bred on agave plantations cultivated for *mezcal*, but in the blue agave fields grown exclusively for tequila, the worms are considered pests that weaken the plants and are destroyed.

IN MEXICO, sangria is often made with lemon-lime soda, such as 7-Up or Sprite. Depending on the region or the restaurant, it may also contain tequila or vodka. We add triple sec, brandy, and a hibiscus-flavored *agua fresca*, which makes this white sangria flowery and bright pink. The wine will always be—and should always be—the most prominent flavor, so it is important to use a good one. Serve the sangria in a pitcher with a long wooden spoon for pulling out the fruit. Its fruitiness makes it a good accompaniment to spicy food.

white hibiscus sangria
SANGRÍA BLANCA CON JAMAICA

MAKES ABOUT 10 CUPS (2½ QUARTS);
SERVES 6 TO 8

- 1 cup cubed fresh fruit, such as oranges, lemons, limes, peeled pears, or peeled apples, or a combination
- 2 (750-ml) bottles white wine, such as chardonnay
- 8 ounces (1 cup) brandy
- 8 ounces (1 cup) freshly squeezed orange juice (about 3 oranges)
- 4 ounces (½ cup) triple sec
- 16 ounces (2 cups) Hibiscus Water (page 4)
- Ice cubes

A day before serving, put the fruit in a 3-quart bowl or pitcher and pour the wine over it. Add the brandy, orange juice, triple sec, and hibiscus water. Stir gently but thoroughly. Cover and refrigerate for at least 1 day and up to 3 days.

Just before serving, stir the sangria. Pour over ice in glasses, adding some fruit to each glass, and serve.

SANGRITA IS A GREAT APPETITE OPENER. We serve it in a shot glass alongside a shot of good *blanco* tequila. The *sangrita* is not a chaser, however. Instead, both drinks are sipped slowly, one after the other. We make the *sangrita* a day ahead of serving to give the flavors time to mingle. You don't have to do this, of course, but you won't be sorry if you do.

tequila with sangrita
TEQUILA Y SANGRITA

MAKES ABOUT 3 CUPS; SERVES 12

> 8 ounces (1 cup) freshly squeezed orange juice (about 3 oranges)
>
> 8 ounces (1 cup) tomato juice
>
> 4 ounces (½ cup) pomegranate juice
>
> 4 ounces (½ cup) bottled Salsa Valentina (see Cook's Note, page 18)
>
> 2 teaspoons kosher salt
>
> Tequila, for serving

A day ahead of serving, in a large glass pitcher or other nonreactive container, mix together the orange juice, tomato juice, pomegranate juice, salsa, and salt. Cover and refrigerate. (The mixture will keep for up to 1 week.)

Just before serving, stir the mixture. Pour into shot glasses and serve with shots of tequila.

SIMILARLY TO OUR WHITE SANGRIA, our red sangria adds brandy and triple sec to the wine and fruit. Our customers like how the jammy flavors of the cabernet sauvignon marry so joyfully with the bite of the citrus. The full-bodied red wine complements the piquancy of our *antojitos*.

red citrus sangria
SANGRÍA ROJA DE CITRICOS

MAKES ABOUT 10 CUPS (2½ QUARTS); SERVES 6

> 1 cup cubed fresh fruit, such as oranges, lemons, limes, peeled pears, or peeled apples, or a combination
>
> 2 (750-ml) bottles full-bodied red wine, such as cabernet sauvignon
>
> 24 ounces (3 cups) freshly squeezed orange juice (about 8 oranges)
>
> 6 ounces (¾ cup) brandy
>
> 4 ounces (½ cup) triple sec
>
> Ice cubes

A day before serving, put the fruit in a 3-quart bowl or pitcher and pour the wine over it. Add the orange juice, brandy, and triple sec. Stir gently but thoroughly. Cover and refrigerate for at least 1 day or up to 3 days.

Just before serving, stir the sangria. Pour over ice in glasses, adding some fruit to each glass, and serve.

ON ONE OF OUR VISITS to Mexico City, Mexican poet Victor Manuel Mendiola took us to his favorite bar in the Colonia Condesa, where we drank a remarkable *mojito* served over shaved ice. At La Palapa, we have taken that inspiration a few steps further. We mix fresh watermelon juice with tequila and mint: the mint cools, the watermelon refreshes, and the *blanco* tequila adds flowery notes. This drink is good served with ice cubes but is even better with shaved ice.

watermelon and tequila mojito
MOJITO DE TEQUILA Y SANDÍA

SERVES 1

5 fresh mint leaves

4 slices lime

1 tablespoon superfine sugar

Ice cubes

2½ ounces (5 tablespoons) blanco tequila, such as Corazón

3 ounces (6 tablespoons) watermelon juice (see Cook's Note)

Shaved ice (optional)

Splash of lemon-lime soda, such as 7-Up

Put the mint leaves, lime slices, and sugar in an 8-ounce glass. Using a muddler or the handle of a wooden spoon, muddle the mint and lime slices, pushing on them to release their juices.

Fill a cocktail shaker with ice cubes, add the tequila and watermelon juice, and shake about 5 times, or until frothy and nicely chilled.

Strain the tequila mixture into the glass, and fill the glass with ice cubes or shaved ice. Top with a splash of soda and serve with a straw.

COOK'S NOTE: *To make the 3 ounces (6 tablespoons) watermelon juice, put about ½ cup peeled, seeded, and coarsely chopped watermelon in a blender and process until smooth.*

OUR VERSION of this hangover cure is similar to a Bloody Mary, with beer in place of the vodka and Salsa Maggi instead of Worcestershire sauce. Any good Mexican brew will work, but we like dark, malty Negra Modelo or Sol, a crisp, light lager. Always sip through a straw, positioning the tip in the middle of the glass so you draw from where the layered flavors converge.

spicy mexican beer cocktail

MICHELADA

SERVES 1

    1½ slices lime
    Piquín Chile Salt (page 138; see Cook's Note)
    Ice cubes
    2 ounces (¼ cup) freshly squeezed lime juice
    1½ ounces (3 tablespoons) bottled Salsa Maggi
    1½ ounces (3 tablespoons) bottled Salsa Valentina (see Cook's Note, page 18)
    1 (12-ounce) bottle Negra Modelo, Sol, or your favorite Mexican beer

Rub the rim of a glass with the whole lime slice. Spread the chile salt on a small plate large enough for the rim of the glass, and dip the rim into the salt to coat.

Fill the glass with ice and add the lime juice and both salsas. Pour about half the beer into the glass. Slit the remaining ½ lime slice partway and balance the slice on the glass rim. Serve with a straw and with the remaining beer on the side.

COOK'S NOTE: *If you want a spicier drink, add a little extra piquín chile powder to the salt mixture.*

A *CHELADA* is just as refreshing and delicious as a *michelada*, but it is much lighter and simpler: fresh lime juice and beer served in a glass with a salted rim. In Mexico City, the names of these two beer cocktails are reversed, with the *chelada* the spicy one. When in doubt, ask which is which.

mexican beer cocktail

CHELADA

SERVES 1

    1½ slices lime
    Kosher salt
    Ice cubes
    2 to 3 ounces (4 to 6 tablespoons) freshly squeezed lime juice
    1 (12-ounce) bottle Mexican light lager, such as Corona, Sol, or Tecate

Rub the rim of a glass with the whole lime slice. Spread the salt on a small plate large enough for the rim of the glass, and dip the rim into the salt to coat.

Fill the glass with ice and add the lime juice. Pour about half the beer into the glass. Slit the remaining ½ lime slice partway and balance the slice on the glass rim. Serve with a straw and with the remaining beer on the side.

IN MARKET STALLS all over Mexico and on the dining table in many Mexican homes, you will find cool, refreshing *aguas frescas*, literally "fresh waters." The Mexican equivalent to iced tea, they are made from different fruits, herbs, and flowers and are ladled out of large, clear jars or poured from pitchers into tall glasses for serving.

Tamarind originated in Africa, migrated to Southeast Asia, and then made its way to Mexico, a route that probably explains why it is more common on Mexico's Pacific coast than its Caribbean side. In Acapulco, you will find tamarind candy, dried salted tamarind, *paletas de tamarindo* (tamarind frozen pops), shrimp in tamarind, and this refreshing *aqua fresca*. At La Palapa, we also use it to infuse tequila and to flavor margaritas. *¡Salud!*

tamarind water
AGUA FRESCA DE TAMARINDO

MAKES ABOUT 8 CUPS; SERVES 6

¼ pound tamarind pulp, or ½ pound tamarind pods (see Cook's Note)

8 cups water

3 tablespoons sugar, or as needed

Ice cubes

If using tamarind pulp, soak the pulp in about 2 cups of the water for about 30 minutes. If using tamarind pods, rinse them in cold water and split open the brittle pods to expose the seeds surrounded by dark flesh. Discard the pods and place the flesh-covered seeds in a bowl. Add about 2 cups of the water, or as needed to cover. Let soak for about 30 minutes.

In a large stockpot, bring the remaining 6 cups water to a boil over high heat. Meanwhile, using a wooden spoon or gloved hands, loosen the soaked pulp and/or flesh-covered seeds with the spoon or your fingers. When the tamarind is loosened, add it and the soaking water to the boiling water.

Let the liquid return to a boil, stirring constantly. Remove from the heat and let cool to lukewarm. Pour the lukewarm tamarind mixture through a fine-mesh sieve into a large bowl. Press on the tamarind pulp with the back of a spoon to extract as much liquid and flavor as possible. Discard the contents of the sieve.

Add the 3 tablespoons sugar to the tamarind liquid and stir to dissolve. Strain again through the sieve into a large jar with a tight-fitting lid. If the flavor is too concentrated, dilute with water or ice. Cover and chill well, then taste and adjust with more sugar, if needed. It will keep in the refrigerator for up to 5 days.

To serve, pour over ice in tall glasses.

COOK'S NOTE: *Look for tamarind pods or blocks of compressed taramind pulp in Mexican, Southeast Asian, or Indian groceries.*

THE WORD *GUACAMOLE* comes from two words in Nahuatl, the language of the Aztecs: *ahuacatl* (avocado) and *molli* (mixture). When possible, we use avocados from the state of Michoacán, where they are grown in volcanic soil in mountainside orchards. The fruits are harvested by hand three times a year at their peak of ripeness, which ensures the guacamole will be creamy and delicious. If you cannot find them, use any flavorful, ripe avocados.

la palapa's classic guacamole
GUACAMOLE DE LA PALAPA

MAKES ABOUT 2 CUPS; SERVES 4 TO 6

2 large avocados, preferably Mexican, halved and pitted

½ sweet onion, such as Vidalia, or 4 spring onions (white part only), finely chopped (see Cook's Note)

½ cup chopped fresh cilantro leaves

1 to 2 serrano or jalapeño chiles, finely chopped (see Cook's Note)

About 1½ tablespoons freshly squeezed lime juice

Kosher salt

Using a tablespoon, scoop out the avocado pulp into a small bowl.

Add the onion, cilantro, chiles, and lime juice. Mix well and season with salt. Taste and adjust with more lime juice if necessary (it both provides flavor and keeps the guacamole from turning brown).

Guacamole tastes best when eaten right away. Or, cover tightly with plastic wrap to prevent discoloring and refrigerate for up to 2 days.

COOK'S NOTE: *If you use spring onions, look for bulbs about 1 inch in diameter. For a spicier guacamole, use 2 chiles and be sure to leave the seeds in them. For less heat, use 1 chile. If you like tomatoes in your guacamole, peel and seed a perfectly ripe tomato, chop it finely, and stir it into the mixture.*

PEACH OR APRICOT is delicious in guacamole, but you can use cubed papaya or mango, too. We also like to pair this salsa with seafood or grilled chicken.

guacamole with tomatillo and peach
GUACAMOLE CON TOMATILLO Y DURAZNO

SERVES 6

- 2 avocados, halved and pitted
- 1 cup cubed, semisoft peaches or apricots
- 4 tomatillos, husked and finely chopped
- 2 jalapeño chiles, seeded, membranes removed, and minced
- 1 small red onion, finely chopped
- 1 cup loosely packed fresh cilantro leaves, chopped (about 1½ bunches)
- 3 tablespoons freshly squeezed lime juice
- 2 teaspoons ancho chile powder
- 1 teaspoon honey
- 2 pinches of freshly ground black pepper
- Kosher salt

Using a tablespoon, scoop out the pulp of 1 of the avocados into a bowl and mash with a fork. Scoop out the pulp of the other avocado, cut the pulp into cubes, and add the cubes to the bowl.

Add the peaches, tomatillos, chiles, onion, cilantro, lime juice, chile powder, honey, and pepper to the avocados and toss gently. Season to taste with salt. Cover tightly to prevent discoloring and refrigerate for about 30 minutes to allow the flavors to mellow before serving. It will keep for up to 2 days.

IN MEXICO, tortilla chips are traditionally served with guacamole. We make our own chips at the restaurants using white, yellow, and blue corn tortillas. We deep-fry them in corn oil to accentuate the flavors of the corn, and season them with cumin, which draws out the sweetness of the corn.

la palapa's tortilla chips
TOTOPOS DE LA PALAPA

SERVES 6

- About 2 tablespoons sea salt or kosher salt
- About 2 tablespoons ground cumin
- 9 (6-inch) corn tortillas, preferably 3 blue, 3 white, and 3 yellow, each cut into 6 wedges
- Corn oil, for deep-frying

In a large, nonreactive bowl, mix together the salt and cumin.

In another large bowl, shake the tortilla wedges to separate them.

In a large, deep sauté pan, pour oil to a depth of at least 2 inches (deep enough to cover the chips as they fry) and heat over medium-high heat to 350°F on a deep-frying thermometer, or until a small piece of tortilla dropped into the hot oil bubbles and crisps within 15 seconds. Fry the tortilla pieces, a few at a time, for 15 to 30 seconds, or until golden and crispy. Using a slotted spoon, transfer the chips to paper towels to drain briefly. Repeat with the remaining tortilla pieces, letting the oil regain temperature between batches.

While the chips are still warm, toss them in the salt-cumin mixture, coating evenly. Serve at room temperature.

IN MEXICAN TOWNS AND CITIES, you often find stands selling these perfect *botanas* tucked under the archways of a plaza. The tostada is essentially an edible plate anchored with beans and then piled high with Mexican condiments. We try new combinations all the time and even make tostadas for New York City street fairs. You can use a single tortilla for each tostada, or cut tortillas into rounds, wedges, or other shapes with a knife or a cookie cutter (see Cook's Note).

traditional tostadas

TOSTADAS TRADICIONALES

MAKES 16 TOSTADAS; SERVES 6 TO 8

1 cup corn oil

16 (6-inch) white corn tortillas

1 teaspoon kosher salt

1 teaspoon ground cumin

2 cups Slow-Cooked Vegetarian Pinto Beans (page 146)

2 cups shredded romaine lettuce

1 cup Fresh Tomato Salsa (page 29)

1 cup La Palapa's Classic Guacamole (page 14)

1 cup Crema Mexicana (page 139)

¼ cup chopped sweet onion, such as Vidalia

¼ cup chopped fresh cilantro leaves

½ cup crumbled queso fresco or finely shredded Monterey Jack cheese

In a deep sauté pan, heat the oil over medium-high heat until a small piece of tortilla dropped into the oil crisps within 15 seconds on the underside. Add 1 tortilla and fry for about 15 seconds on the first side, or until it starts to curl. Turn and fry on the second side for 15 seconds longer, or until crisp. Be careful not to overcook. Using a slotted spoon or tongs, transfer to paper towels to drain. Let the oil regain temperature after frying each tortilla. While still warm, spread the fried tortillas in a single layer on baking sheets or platters and season with salt and cumin.

In a sauté pan, heat the beans over medium heat, stirring constantly to prevent sticking, for about 3 minutes, or until hot.

Spread each tostada with about 2 tablespoons beans and top with 2 tablespoons lettuce, 1 tablespoon salsa, 1 tablespoon guacamole, a dollop of *crema*, and a little onion, cilantro, and cheese. Serve immediately.

COOK'S NOTE: *To make small tostadas as canapés for a fiesta, cut the tortillas into 3-inch rounds with a cookie cutter, to make 32 medium-size tostadas, or cut each tortilla into wedge-shaped quarters, to make 64 small tostadas. Separate the pieces and fry them in small batches so they don't stick together, and then divide the toppings evenly among them.*

IN NORTHERN MEXICO, where wheat is grown, quesadillas are made with large flour tortillas and filled with tangy *queso Chihuahua*. Farther south in Oaxaca, cooks make tortillas with corn *masa* and fill them with creamy *queso Oaxaca*. In the Yucatán, with its free port and easy access to the Dutch Caribbean, cooks routinely use Edam cheese. At La Palapa, we use a mix of cheeses, so each bite carries the saltiness of *queso añejo*, the creamy tang of *queso fresco*, and the smoothness of Monterey Jack, and we serve them with a trio of *salsas de mesa*. You can put out guacamole, too. Quesadillas taste best piping hot, but are also good at room temperature.

three-cheese quesadillas
QUESADILLAS DE TRES QUESOS

SERVES 6

- 12 (6-inch) corn or flour tortillas
- ½ cup finely shredded Monterey Jack cheese
- ½ cup crumbled queso fresco or ricotta salata cheese
- ½ cup grated queso añejo
- ½ cup Fresh Tomato Salsa (page 29)
- ½ cup Charred Serrano Chile Salsa (page 22)
- ½ cup La Palapa's Tomatillo Salsa (page 25)

Heat a large griddle or cast-iron or nonstick skillet over medium heat until a few drops of water flicked onto the surface sizzle on contact. (Because you make quesadillas in batches, you may want to use more than 1 pan.) Lay 2 or 3 tortillas on the griddle and warm on each side for about 20 seconds, or until soft enough to fold easily over the filling.

Put 2 teaspoons of each cheese in the center of each tortilla and fold the tortilla in half, as if making a turnover. Warm for about 20 seconds longer, or until the cheese closest to the griddle starts to melt. Turn the folded quesadilla over and heat the other side for about 20 seconds, or until all the cheese melts. As the quesadillas are done, transfer them to a platter (see Cook's Note).

Serve the quesadillas warm with the salsas.

COOK'S NOTE: *To keep cooked quesadillas warm, cover them with a dry kitchen towel. Do not cover them with a plate or aluminum foil, or they will steam. If you have no choice but to use foil, poke vent holes in it. If the quesadillas cool off too much, reheat in a microwave oven on high power for 12 to 15 seconds.*

WE SAMPLED THIS *BOTANA* on the Riviera Maya, as the pristine swath of the Mexican Caribbean south of Cancún is called. We came across a bar on the edge of the white sand beach at the Maroma Resort and quickly befriended the bartender, Enrique. The salty, spicy, tart green olives are the perfect accompaniment to a Mexican Beer Cocktail (page 11), so we wheedled this recipe out of Enrique. You will have to plan ahead for this one, so the olives can spend some time in the marinade.

seasoned olives
ACEITUNAS SAZONADAS

MAKES ABOUT 4 CUPS

- 4 cups manzanilla olives
- ¼ cup freshly squeezed lime juice (about 2 limes)
- ¼ cup bottled Salsa Valentina or Salsa Búfalo (see Cook's Note)
- 3 tablespoons bottled Salsa Maggi
- 1 tablespoon finely chopped fresh oregano leaves

Drain the olives, but keep them in their original jar or put them in a clean quart jar. Add the lime juice and both salsas. Stir well or cover and shake well to coat the olives.

Let the olives marinate in the refrigerator for at least 3 hours, though they taste best when allowed to marinate for about 1 week. They will keep for up to 3 weeks. Serve in a shallow bowl, garnished with the oregano.

COOK'S NOTE: *These hot sauces are sold in Mexican stores and on the Internet at www.mexgrocer.com and other sites selling Mexican ingredients.*

AT CANTINAS ALL OVER MEXICO, bartenders proudly serve their favorite *botanas*, or snacks. Recipes are closely guarded, and patrons are often asked to guess the secret ingredient that makes the *botana* of a particular *cantinero* special. Roasted peanuts are a common bar snack in Mexico, and this version is among the best. Our bartenders happily refill bowls with these spicy, addictive nuts.

spicy roasted peanuts
CACAHUATES ENCHILADOS

MAKES 1 POUND

- 1 pound salted, roasted peanuts
- ¼ cup freshly squeezed lime juice (about 2 limes)
- 2 tablespoons kosher salt
- 2 tablespoons sweet Spanish paprika
- 2 teaspoons piquín chile powder
- ½ teaspoon ground cumin

Spread the peanuts in a single layer in a sauté pan and cook over low heat, stirring often, for 1 to 2 minutes, or until aromatic.

Add the lime juice, toss to mix, and while still damp from the lime juice, add the salt, paprika, chile powder, and cumin. Toss well to distribute the spices and evaporate the lime juice.

Transfer the peanuts to a bowl and let cool completely before serving. The peanuts will keep in a lidded container at room temperature for up to 1 week.

2 *salsas de mesa*
SALSAS FOR THE TABLE

WE USUALLY USE SERRANO CHILES for this recipe, but if you like a spicier salsa, toss a few fiery habaneros into the mix. Habaneros are popular throughout the Yucatán, and when we travel there, we always order a *salsa picante* (spicy-hot salsa) to give our taste buds a jolt. One of our favorites is made at Picos, a tiny seafood restaurant on Isla Mujeres, a small island a short ferry trip from Cancún. We get off the ferry, bags in hand, and head directly for Picos for whole steamed snapper served with a mind-blowing salsa, a margarita, and a warm smile.

charred serrano chile salsa

SALSA DE CHILE SERRANO TORREADO

MAKES ABOUT 4 CUPS

1 pound serrano chiles (see Cook's Note)
1 cup distilled white vinegar
1 cup rice vinegar
About 2 tablespoons kosher salt

Using a dry griddle, grill pan, or cast-iron skillet, and working in batches to avoid crowding, char the chiles over medium heat, turning them with tongs or a long-handled fork to color evenly on all sides. When the skins have blistered and blackened, lift the chiles from the pan and set aside. As you work, try not to breathe in the hot chile vapors, which can irritate your throat and eyes.

Pour both vinegars into a blender or food processor, add the salt, and pulse 3 or 4 times to mix. Add the chiles and pulse until chopped into ½-inch pieces.

Let cool completely before serving. To store, transfer to a glass jar or other nonreactive container, cover tightly, and refrigerate for up to 1 month.

COOK'S NOTE: *For a searing-hot salsa, substitute habanero chiles for all of the serranos. Habaneros are extremely hot, so take special care when charring because of their powerful vapors. When you work with habaneros, wear gloves, never touch your eyes or mouth, and wash your hands immediately afterward. We have been known to wrap our hands in plastic wrap or cover them with plastic bags when gloves were not available. This is one fierce chile!*

THIS MAY NOT MEET YOUR CRITERIA for salsa, but once you try the smooth, creamy mixture, you will want to make it all the time. We begin by roasting the tomatoes, onions, and garlic on the stove top in just enough oil and for just enough time to bring out their sweetness before we blend them with the toasted chiles. The result is a sweet, mellow, spicy salsa that is amazing with pork, beef, shrimp, or chicken; rolled into tortillas with vegetables or sliced meats; or served alongside our Three-Cheese Quesadillas (page 17).

árbol chile and roasted tomato salsa

SALSA DE CHILE DE ÁRBOL

MAKES 2 TO 3 CUPS

- 1½ cups plus 1 tablespoon corn oil
- 6 plum tomatoes
- 1 large onion (about ½ pound), coarsely chopped
- 2 cloves garlic
- 6 árbol chiles
- Kosher salt

In a 2-quart saucepan, heat the 1½ cups oil over medium-low heat. Add the tomatoes, onion, and garlic and cook, stirring occasionally with a wooden spoon, for about 20 minutes, or until the vegetables soften. Remove from the heat. Remove the tomatoes from the oil and set aside. Reserve the onion, garlic, and oil in the pan.

Meanwhile, in a skillet, heat the remaining 1 tablespoon oil over medium-high heat. Add the chiles and toast them, tossing constantly, for about 15 seconds, or just until fragrant. Be careful not to scorch them. Remove from the heat.

When the tomatoes and chiles are cool enough to handle, core the tomatoes and remove the stems from the chiles. Add the tomatoes, chiles, and the contents of the saucepan to a blender or food processor and process until smooth and the consistency of heavy cream.

Return the puree to the saucepan and stir gently with a wooden spoon over medium heat for about 3 minutes, or until the salsa emulsifies, is creamy, and turns a burnt orange. Season to taste with salt.

Let the salsa cool before serving as a *salsa de mesa*. If you want to spoon it directly over steak, chicken, or shrimp, serve it warm. To store, transfer to a glass jar or other nonreactive container, cover tightly, and refrigerate for up to 1 month.

SOMETIMES CALLED "MEXICAN TOMATOES," tomatillos are in fact related to the gooseberry. They are harvested at their peak of ripeness and are sold with their papery husks intact, which must be removed before using. Look for firm, unblemished fruits and store them in the refrigerator, where they will keep for up to 1 month. Tomatillos are particularly prized in central Mexico, where they are used in raw and cooked salsas and are cooked in green moles. This uncooked tomatillo salsa, with its citrus tang, is perfect with fried fish or shellfish or with cheese quesadillas. It also shows up in *taquerias* all over Mexico—and at La Palapa, as well.

la palapa's tomatillo salsa
SALSA VERDE DE LA PALAPA

MAKES ABOUT 2 CUPS

1 pound tomatillos, husks removed and coarsely chopped

10 to 12 sprigs cilantro, coarsely chopped

1 or 2 jalapeño or serrano chiles, stemmed

About ¼ cup water, or as needed

½ cup finely chopped sweet onion, such as Vidalia

Kosher salt

In a blender or food processor, combine the tomatillos, cilantro, and chiles. Use 1 or 2 chiles, depending on the degree of spiciness you want. Pulse, adding the water a little at a time, until the salsa reaches a consistency you like. It should be coarsely pureed.

Transfer the salsa to a nonreactive bowl and stir in the onion. Season to taste with salt. Use right away, or cover and refrigerate for up to 5 days.

WHAT IS A PALAPA?

Over the years, we have been asked how we chose the name for our restaurants. *Palapas* are the palm-thatched umbrellas and little houses (*casitas*) found along beaches in Mexico. They are refuges from the sun where you can relax and watch the sparkling blue waves, drink an ice-cold *cerveza*, and bite into a savory, spicy *antojito*. The palm thatch is also used for the handsome, sweet-smelling canopies found on homes in the Pacific states of Guerrero and Oaxaca—thatched dwellings that have always looked welcoming to us. We want our guests to feel the same way about our restaurants.

THIS SALSA IS TYPICAL of the colonial town of Guadalajara, where street vendors cook delicious foods right in the central plaza, or *zócalo*, and each has his or her own version of a spicy blended salsa for selling with tacos. It goes particularly well with chorizo and steak tacos, and at La Palapa, we serve it with skirt steak, chorizo, guacamole, grilled nopal cactus, and pickled red onions, wrapped together in a warm tortilla. It is also great served alongside a soft poached egg perched on top of a *chalupa*.

mortar-crushed tomato salsa

SALSA TAPATÍA DE MOLCAJETE

MAKES ABOUT 4 CUPS

2 cups water

6 plum tomatoes

3 tomatillos, husks removed

2 or 3 jalapeño chiles, stemmed

2 cloves garlic

1 cup finely chopped fresh cilantro leaves (about 1½ bunches)

1 teaspoon ground cumin

1 teaspoon kosher salt

¼ teaspoon freshly ground black pepper

In a nonreactive saucepan, bring the water to a simmer over medium-high heat. Add the tomatoes, tomatillos, chiles (use all 3 chiles if you like a spicy salsa), and garlic. Let the water return to a simmer and cook for about 2 minutes, or until the tomato skins loosen. Remove from the heat.

Add the cilantro, cumin, salt, and pepper and stir gently. Drain the contents of the pan into a colander placed over a bowl, and set the solids and liquid aside separately.

When the tomatoes and tomatillos are cool enough to handle, peel and chop coarsely. Then coarsely chop the chiles and garlic. For less heat, scrape the seeds and membranes from the chiles before you chop them.

Working in batches, mash the tomatoes, tomatillos, chiles, and garlic in a mortar with a pestle. Add small amounts of the cooking liquid to keep the salsa moist and easy to mash. Or, process the ingredients in a food processor until smooth.

Transfer to a bowl, let cool, and serve. Or, transfer to a glass jar or other nonreactive container, cover tightly, and refrigerate for up to 1 week.

BARBARA HAS FOND MEMORIES of a pristine lake in the town of Valle de Bravo, a two-and-a-half-hour drive from Mexico City, where she picnicked on cold roast pork loin with a fresh avocado salsa very much like this one. The zesty sauce was perfect for a lunch at the lakeside, with the bright Mexican sun making the water dance and shine. At La Palapa, we add tomatillos to the salsa, which provide a complementary sour edge to the rich avocados. If you prefer a spicier salsa, use both chiles and leave their seeds and membranes intact.

avocado-tomatillo salsa

GUACASALSA

MAKES ABOUT 2 CUPS

- 1 avocado, halved and pitted
- 6 tomatillos, husks removed, cored, and quartered
- 1 to 2 jalapeño chiles, seeded and membranes removed
- 1 cup loosely packed chopped fresh cilantro leaves (about 1½ bunches)
- ¼ cup chopped sweet onion, such as Vidalia (see Cook's Note)
- 1 clove garlic, coarsely chopped
- ¼ cup freshly squeezed lime juice (about 2 limes)
- Kosher salt and freshly ground black pepper

Using a tablespoon, scoop out the pulp of the avocado into a food processor or blender.

Add the tomatillos, chiles, cilantro, onion, and garlic and process for about 10 seconds, or until creamy but still chunky.

Transfer the salsa to a nonreactive bowl, stir in the lime juice, and season with salt and pepper. Cover and chill well before serving. For optimal flavor, refrigerate the salsa for no more than 4 hours before serving. However, it still tastes good if stored in a tightly covered glass jar or other nonreactive container in the refrigerator for up to 3 days.

COOK'S NOTE: *We use Vidalia onions for this salsa because they are closest to the mild onions grown near Mexico City. Yellow and red onions are too overpowering. But if you cannot find a sweet onion, rinse the chopped onion under cold running water for about 30 seconds to remove some of its sharpness.*

PICO DE GALLO MEANS "rooster's beak" in Spanish and refers to the colors in this salsa: red and green for the cock's feathers and white for his beak. It is also known as *salsa mexicana* or *salsa bandera* because red, white, and green are the colors of the Mexican flag. We like to serve this salsa in the summer when we can get tomatoes like the ones we buy at the *tianguiz* (outdoor market) on the street where Barbara's mother lives in Mexico City. Here in New York, we use tomatoes from Margaritte's country garden—tomatoes so fresh they still seem warm from the summer sun.

fresh tomato salsa

PICO DE GALLO

MAKES ABOUT 4 CUPS

- 2 cups diced, seeded ripe tomatoes (about 6 tomatoes)
- 1 cup diced sweet onion, such as Vidalia (about 1 onion)
- 3 to 5 jalapeño chiles, seeded, membranes removed, and cut into ¼-inch dice
- 3 tablespoons freshly squeezed lime juice
- ½ cup finely chopped fresh cilantro leaves
- Kosher salt

Put the tomatoes, onion, and chiles in a nonreactive bowl. Stir in the lime juice and then the cilantro. Season to taste with salt.

Set the salsa aside at room temperature for about 1 hour to give the salt time to pull the moisture from the vegetables so the flavors blend. Cover and refrigerate for at least 2 hours or up to 8 hours before serving. Serve chilled or at room temperature.

Cinco de Mayo

On this exciting day, we have one gigantic fiesta. We decorate the restaurants with beautiful etched paper (called *papel picado*) and Mexican flags, and mariachi bands supply the music on both the east and west sides of Manhattan. Each band has eight musicians who wear silver-studded *charro* outfits and wide-brimmed hats and often sing as well as play lively music. Everyone loves the music, the food, the drinks, and the balmy May weather.

We serve dishes and beverages that share colors with the Mexican flag: red, white, and green. For example, our *sangrita* is red, the tequila is white, and we serve them with a shot of lime juice for a traditional Mexican trio of shots. When you rim the margarita with *piquín* chile–laced salt, all of the colors of the Mexican flag adorn the cocktail. Our crispy *chalupas* are garnished with chorizo, which is red; *crema*, which is white; and tomatillo salsa, which is green. The *taquitos* are in the style of Puebla, which is where the battle that Cinco de Mayo commemorates was fought and won by the Mexicans. When you serve the quesadillas, make sure the accompanying salsas reflect the colors of the flag, too.

SERVES 10 TO 12

FOR THIS CHUNKY SALSA, the ingredients are lightly roasted and then briefly blended. We use round, reddish brown *cascabel* chiles, which are sweet and spicy and shaped like a rattle or maraca. They even make a little sound if you shake them. Because *cascabel* chiles are not very hot, you don't need to seed the chiles to tone down the heat. *Árbol* chiles are a good substitute, though the salsa will be much more fiery. Serve with steak, quesadillas, tacos, and even scrambled eggs.

rustic cascabel chile and tomatillo salsa

SALSA MACHA DE CHILE CASCABEL

MAKES ABOUT 2 CUPS

12 to 14 tomatillos, husks removed
1 large clove garlic
8 cascabel chiles
1 cup water
⅛ teaspoon ground cumin
Kosher salt

Heat a dry griddle, grill pan, or cast-iron skillet over medium-high heat. Roast the tomatillos and garlic, turning several times, for about 5 minutes, or until charred on all sides but not fully cooked through. Remove from the pan and set aside.

Add the chiles to the same hot pan and roast, turning often so they do not burn, for about 30 seconds on each side. Remove the chiles from the pan and set aside to cool.

In a blender or food processor, combine the tomatillos, garlic, and water and pulse to chop coarsely. You want some texture remaining.

When the chiles are cool enough to handle, crumble them into the blender, add the cumin, and pulse to mix. Season to taste with salt.

Let the salsa rest at room temperature before serving for at least 2 hours or up to 8 hours to allow time for the flavors to develop. Or, transfer to a glass jar or other nonreactive container, cover tightly, and refrigerate for up to 4 days.

YOU CAN USE THIS tangy salsa at room temperature with tacos and quesadillas and hot with enchiladas or huevos rancheros. We also use it to season our chicken tamales (see page 67).

cooked tomatillo salsa

SALSA VERDE COCIDA

MAKES ABOUT 2 CUPS

10 to 12 tomatillos, husks removed

1 or 2 jalapeño or serrano chiles, stemmed

½ cup finely chopped white onion

4 cloves garlic, finely chopped

1 teaspoon sugar

1 teaspoon kosher salt

1 teaspoon ground cumin

¼ teaspoon ground cloves

⅛ teaspoon freshly ground black pepper

½ cup chopped fresh cilantro leaves

¼ cup corn oil

In a small stockpot, combine the tomatillos, chiles (use both chiles if you like spicy salsas), onion, garlic, sugar, salt, cumin, cloves, and pepper and add water to cover. Bring to a boil over medium heat and boil for about 10 minutes, or until the bright green tomatillos turn a dull olive green and are cooked through. Remove from the heat.

Drain the contents of the pot into a colander placed over a bowl, and set the solids and cooking liquid aside separately. Working in batches, transfer the solids to a blender and process until smooth, adding the reserved cooking liquid as needed to achieve a salsa with the consistency of a creamed vegetable soup. Add the cilantro and continue to process until the cilantro is pureed.

Return the puree to the pot, add the oil, and bring to a boil over medium heat. Turn off the heat, then taste and adjust the seasoning with salt, if needed. Let cool completely and serve. Or, transfer to a glass jar or other nonreactive container, cover tightly, and refrigerate for up to 5 days.

WHEN POET JENNIFER CLEMENT arrived on a visit from Mexico City during our first year of operation, she brought us a salsa similar to this one. It has been on our menu ever since. We liked the combination of the bright heat of the *árbol* chiles and the creaminess of the peanut butter. When we paired it with a tender steak, we were in heaven. We also found it was celestial with quesadillas, beef-filled *chalupas*, rice cooked with tomatoes, and sautéed Swiss chard.

peanut and árbol chile salsa

SALSA DE CACAHUATE Y CHILE DE ÁRBOL

MAKES ABOUT 2 CUPS

1 pound plum tomatoes, chopped

½ cup chopped white onion

4 cloves garlic, finely chopped

¼ teaspoon dried thyme, or 1 teaspoon fresh thyme leaves

1 tablespoon kosher salt

¼ teaspoon freshly ground white pepper

About ¾ cup plus 1 tablespoon corn oil

¼ cup stemmed, chopped árbol chiles (about 15 chiles)

½ cup creamy peanut butter

2 tablespoons warm water, or as needed

¼ cup salted, roasted peanuts

In a 2-quart saucepan, combine the tomatoes, onion, garlic, thyme, salt, and pepper. Add enough of the ¾ cup oil to cover the ingredients, place the pan over medium heat, and bring to a simmer. Cook for about 10 minutes, or until the onion softens and all the vegetables are well blended.

In a skillet, heat the remaining 1 tablespoon oil over medium heat. Add the chiles and fry for about 30 seconds, or until soft and fragrant. Add the chiles and frying oil to the saucepan, stir to mix, then immediately remove from the heat and set aside to cool.

Transfer the cooled tomato mixture to a food processor and process until a thick, creamy sauce forms. Or, working in batches, process in a blender, then return all of the processed mixture to the blender.

Add the peanut butter and pulse to mix well. Add the 2 tablespoons water and process until smooth and thinned to a nice consistency, adding more water as needed.

Transfer to a bowl, garnish with the peanuts, and serve warm. Or, transfer to a glass jar or other nonreactive container, cover tightly, and refrigerate for up to 1 week. Just before serving, reheat gently until warm and garnish with the peanuts.

THIS IS A WONDERFULLY VERSATILE SALSA, which makes it a great favorite with us. You can adjust the spiciness by adding more chiles or adobo, or more of both. Serve the *crema* as a bright, creamy dip with tortilla chips; try it with seafood, meats, or chicken; or dollop it on sandwiches or tacos. We serve it with our fish tacos (see page 51).

chipotle crema
CREMA DE CHIPOTLE

MAKES ABOUT 2½ CUPS

    3 chipotles en adobo
    1 teaspoon freshly squeezed lime juice
    1¾ cups Crema Mexicana (page 139)
    ¼ teaspoon ground cumin
    ¼ cup finely chopped fresh cilantro leaves
    Kosher salt and freshly ground black pepper

In a blender, combine the chiles and lime juice and process until smooth. Transfer to a nonreactive bowl, add the *crema* and cumin, and stir until the salsa is a uniform rose color. Fold in the cilantro and season with salt and pepper.

Serve immediately, or transfer to a glass jar or other nonreactive container, cover tightly, and refrigerate for up to 5 days.

ONE OF THE HOTTEST CHILES is the habanero, which has mistakenly been called a Chinese pepper, although it is most likely native to the Amazon Basin and did not find its way to China until the seventeenth or eighteenth century. The largest crop of habaneros is grown in the Yucatán, home to the Mayans, which explains this salsa's name: *xnipec*. Pronounce the *x* like "sh" and the word will roll off your tongue just as the salsa does. In the Yucatán, main dishes are not extremely spicy, so home cooks put this fiery salsa on the table and let diners add the amount of heat they want.

pickled onion and habanero salsa
SALSA XNIPEC

MAKES ABOUT 1 CUP

    1 cup thinly sliced red onion
    1 cup freshly squeezed lime juice
       (about 8 limes)
    1 tablespoon finely chopped habanero
       chile (see Cook's Note, page 22), or
       2 tablespoons finely chopped jalapeño chile
    1 teaspoon kosher salt

In a nonreactive bowl, stir together the onion, lime juice, chile, and salt. Cover the bowl and refrigerate for 3 hours to allow the flavors to blend.

Taste a little of the pickling juice and adjust the amount of salt, then serve. Or, transfer to a glass jar or other nonreactive container, cover tightly, and refrigerate for up to 1 week.

LA SIRENA

IN THE STATE OF GUERRERO, on Mexico's Pacific coast, this colorful ceviche is made with marlin, a slightly oily fish caught by game fishermen. Barbara's father made a family tradition of fishing for these big, beautiful fish, and she recalls the bittersweet moment when she hooked her first *pez sierra* and saw its gorgeous rainbow fin rise above the sea. Despite her ambivalence about fishing and then eating the catch, we are both avid fans of this ceviche. At La Palapa, we find that salmon approximates the rich taste of marlin—and is easier to acquire.

salmon ceviche with fresh mango salsa
CEVICHE DE SALMÓN CON PICO DE MANGO

SERVES 6

1 pound wild salmon fillets,
    cut into 1-inch cubes

1 cup freshly squeezed lime juice
    (about 8 limes)

3 tomatillos, husks removed and diced

1 plum tomato, diced

½ cup diced Vidalia onion, spring onions,
    or scallions (white part only)

1 cup coarsely chopped, peeled mango,
    papaya, or peach or coarsely chopped,
    unpeeled nectarine

1 tablespoon ancho chile powder

1 tablespoon honey

1½ teaspoons kosher salt

2 jalapeño chiles

6 thin slices tomatillo (optional)

6 fresh cilantro leaves

La Palapa's Tortilla Chips (page 15)

Put the salmon in a glass or other nonreactive dish and toss with ¾ cup of the lime juice. Cover and refrigerate for at least 4 hours or up to 8 hours. The fish should be opaque. Drain and discard the lime juice.

Transfer the salmon to a nonreactive bowl and add the remaining ¼ cup lime juice, the diced tomatillos, tomato, onion, mango, chile powder, honey, and salt. Stir gently to mix well.

If you prefer a mild salsa, trim off the stem end of the chiles and scrape out the membranes and seeds. For a spicy salsa, leave the membranes and seeds intact. Cut the chiles into thin rounds. Add to the bowl and stir gently.

Cover and chill for at least 1 hour or up to 8 hours to allow the flavors to blend.

Serve the ceviche in chilled martini glasses or goblets. Garnish each serving with a tomatillo slice, cut to the center and folded into a twist, and a cilantro leaf. Serve the tortilla chips on the side. The marriage of textures—the crunchy chips and the smooth fish—is irresistible.

Día de las Madres | MOTHER'S DAY

In Mexico, Mother's Day is a national holiday. Nowhere are mothers more honored, and the day begins early with children serenading their mothers with song. We like Mother's Day, too. Not only are both of us moms, but we also enjoy the idea of celebrating families. We offer a special brunch menu for the happy holiday, and add a little elegance to it by serving duck breast tostadas with a delicious fig sauce. The fish-topped *chalupas* with a pumpkin seed sauce are a bit time-consuming to prepare but worth the effort. And Mother's Day is not complete without a sweet dessert. Try our flan. It's out of this world!

Sangria is a light, festive beverage, and our white sangria, which actually has a rosy tint, is perfect for a Mother's Day celebration.

SERVES 10

THIS SIMPLE FLAN is similar to one you might find in any Mexican home. We got the recipe from our friend Juan Torres, who in turn got it from his mother who lives in the state of Morelos. Use heady, fragrant Mexican vanilla extract and soft, mildly smoky Mexican cinnamon for the most authentic flavor.

mexico city–style kahlúa and vanilla flan
FLAN DEL ESTADO DE MEXICO

SERVES 10

- 2 cups whole milk
- 2 cups half-and-half
- 4 cups sugar
- 1 (4-inch) stick Mexican cinnamon
- 1 teaspoon pure vanilla extract, preferably Mexican
- 5 large egg yolks
- 3 large whole eggs
- ⅓ cup coffee liqueur, such as Kahlúa or Tia Maria, or brewed espresso

Preheat the oven to 325°F. Position an oven rack in the center of the oven.

In a large saucepan, combine the milk, half-and-half, 1 cup of the sugar, and the cinnamon stick and bring to a boil over medium-high heat. Reduce the heat and simmer briskly for about 3 minutes, stirring until the sugar dissolves. Remove from the heat, add the vanilla extract, and let the mixture cool. Strain through a fine-mesh sieve into a bowl. Discard the cinnamon stick.

In another bowl, whisk together the egg yolks, whole eggs, and liqueur. Whisk in about ½ cup of the hot milk mixture to temper the eggs, then slowly add the remaining milk mixture, whisking until smooth.

Arrange 10 (8-ounce) custard cups, ramekins, or similar molds in a deep roasting pan large enough to hold them without touching. In a heavy saucepan, heat the remaining 3 cups sugar over medium heat, stirring until the sugar melts. Bring the sugar to a boil and boil, without stirring, for 5 to 8 minutes, or until it caramelizes and turns golden brown. Remove from the heat and divide the caramel evenly among the molds. Use a heavy pot holder or oven mitt and take great care: the caramel is very hot.

Ladle equal amounts of the custard into the molds, filling them nearly to the top. Put the pan on the oven rack and carefully pour hot water into the pan to come halfway up the sides of the molds. Bake for about 40 minutes, or until the custards are set but still a little wobbly in the center when a mold is shaken.

Remove the pan from the oven and let the flans cool in the water bath. Remove the molds from the water bath and refrigerate for at least 1 hour to chill well, or for up to 3 days. If holding for more than 1 hour, cover each mold with plastic wrap.

To serve, run a thin knife blade between the custard and the rim of the mold, pressing the knife against the mold and not the custard. Invert an individual serving plate on top of a mold, and invert the flan and the plate together. Carefully lift the mold off the flan so the caramel syrup drips down its sides. Repeat with the other molds. Serve immediately.

THE ADDITION OF CAPERS AND OLIVES to this simple ceviche from the port of Veracruz reminds us of Spain's influence on the Mexican table. To cut down on the preparation time—or if you don't like the idea of serving shrimp "cooked" only in lime juice—poach the shrimp in boiling salted water just until they turn pink, drain, cool, cover with lime juice, and refrigerate for up to 1 hour, or until well chilled, then continue as directed.

veracruz-style spicy shrimp ceviche

CEVICHE DE CAMARÓN PICOSITO VERACRUZANO

SERVES 6

COOKED TOMATO SALSA
1 tablespoon corn oil
2 cloves garlic
5 plum tomatoes, halved
Leaves from ½ bunch Mexican oregano
1 teaspoon sugar
Kosher salt and freshly ground black pepper

CEVICHE
1 pound medium shrimp, peeled and deveined
About 3 cups freshly squeezed lime juice
    (about 24 limes)
2 cups Fresh Tomato Salsa (page 29)
⅓ cup sliced large green pitted olives
    (about 15 olives)
2 avocados, halved, pitted, peeled, and cubed
⅓ cup nonpareil capers, rinsed and drained

GARNISHES
1 avocado, halved and pitted
6 sprigs cilantro
1 lime, sliced into 6 rounds

To make the cooked salsa, in a 2-quart saucepan, heat the oil over medium heat. Add the garlic and cook for 1 to 2 minutes, or until softened but not colored. Take care not to overcook.

Add the tomatoes, oregano, and sugar and cook, stirring, for about 10 minutes, or until the mixture has a saucelike consistency. Remove from the heat and let cool slightly.

Transfer the salsa to a blender and process until smooth. Season with salt and pepper. Transfer to a glass or other nonreactive container and refrigerate for at least 1 hour, or until chilled.

To make the ceviche, in a nonreactive bowl, gently mix the shrimp and lime juice. Cover tightly and refrigerate for at least 6 hours or up to 12 hours to give the shrimp time to "cook" in the lime juice.

Remove the shrimp from the lime juice with a slotted spoon and transfer them to a nonreactive bowl. Add the fresh salsa, olives, avocados, and capers and mix gently.

To serve, spoon ¼ cup of the cooked salsa into the bottom of each of 6 serving dishes. Divide the ceviche evenly among the dishes, then top each serving with about 1 tablespoon of the cooked salsa. To garnish the servings, peel each avocado half, and cut each half lengthwise into 3 wedges. Thinly slice 1 wedge, and fan the slices over a serving. Repeat with the remaining avocado wedges. Garnish each serving with a cilantro sprig and a lime slice and serve right away.

THE MARINADE USED HERE is typical of the marinades made in Mérida, in the Yucatán. Cooks there use a bitter orange called *naranja agria*. The trees thrive in the central courtyards of haciendas throughout the city and the surrounding countryside, and home cooks need only wander out the kitchen door to pick the sharp-flavored fruits for their recipes. We rarely have access to the astringent oranges of Mérida, so we approximate their taste by blending freshly squeezed orange juice, lime juice, and grapefruit juice.

la palapa's fish tacos

TACOS DE PESCADO DE LA PALAPA

MAKES 12 TACOS; SERVES 6

CHILES

3 tablespoons corn oil

3 pasilla chiles, cut into 1-inch-thick rounds

1 teaspoon kosher salt

MARINADE

¼ cup achiote paste

¾ cup freshly squeezed orange juice (about 2 oranges)

¼ cup freshly squeezed lime juice (about 2 limes)

¼ cup freshly squeezed grapefruit juice (about 1 grapefruit)

¼ cup Árbol Chile and Roasted Tomato Salsa (page 24)

½ small white onion

1 tablespoon honey

1 clove garlic

1 teaspoon kosher salt

1 cup olive oil

1 pound tilapia, red snapper, catfish, or other flaky, white fish fillets

Kosher salt and freshly ground black pepper

3 tablespoons corn oil

12 (6-inch) corn tortillas

12 romaine lettuce leaves from heart, each about 6 inches long and 2 inches wide

½ cup Avocado-Tomatillo Salsa (page 28)

½ cup Chipotle Crema (page 36)

To prepare the chiles, in a sauté pan, heat the corn oil over medium heat. Add the chiles and cook, stirring, for about 1 minute, or until they plump up and are crisp. Take care they do not scorch. Using a slotted spoon, transfer to a bowl, season with salt, and let cool.

To make the marinade, put all of the ingredients except the olive oil in a blender and blend until liquefied. With the motor running, add the oil in a steady stream, processing until the mixture is emulsified. Set aside in a nonreactive container. You will have about 3 cups.

CONTINUED ▶

Pat the fish fillets dry, season them with salt and pepper, lay them in a shallow, nonreactive bowl, and add about ½ cup of the marinade, or just enough to coat them. Cover and refrigerate for at least 1 hour and no more than 2 hours. Remove the fillets from the marinade and pat dry. Discard the marinade.

In a nonstick skillet, heat the corn oil over medium-high heat. Sear the fillets, turning once, for about 2 minutes on each side, or just until they are opaque and flake easily when prodded with a fork.

Add ½ cup of the marinade, scrape the pan bottom to deglaze, and cook for about 2 minutes longer, or until the marinade thickens. Don't worry if the fillets break into pieces. Transfer the fillets to a plate, and drizzle any marinade in the pan over the top. Cut the fillets into 2-inch pieces. (Reserve the remaining 2 cups marinade for another use. It will keep in the refrigerator for up to 2 days.)

Warm the tortillas (see page 130). Cut twelve 6-inch squares of parchment paper. Lay a tortilla on a parchment square. Put about 2 tablespoons fish down the center, and top with a lettuce leaf and 3 or 4 chile rounds. Using the parchment, fold the tortilla in half and transfer to a serving plate. Repeat until all the ingredients are used, then arrange the tacos side by side so that they hold one another up. Serve the salsa and *crema* on the side.

THIS HOME-STYLE RECIPE is adapted from one taught to us by our head chef, Domingo Torres, who remembers eating it as a child in Mexico. Central Mexico is filled with rivers, streams, and lakes, and freshwater fish, such as the catfish used here, are popular there. The addition of mayonnaise echoes the early influence of French cuisine on Mexican cooking. We like to make these tamales in the summertime, when we save the husks from fresh ears of corn. Hearts of Palm Salad with Fresh Oregano Vinaigrette (page 110) is a good accompaniment.

spiced catfish and nopal cactus tamales
TAMALES DE VAGRE

SERVES 6

13 fresh corn husks

2 nopal cactus paddles (see Cook's Note)

⅓ cup distilled white vinegar

1 pound catfish fillets, cut into 6 equal strips each 1 to 2 inches wide

¼ cup mayonnaise

¼ cup thinly sliced onion

12 paper-thin slices jalapeño chile

6 epazote leaves

1 teaspoon sweet Spanish paprika

Preheat the oven to 375°F. Fill a large pot three-fourths full with water and bring to a boil over high heat. Tear 1 corn husk into ½-inch-wide strips. You will need 6 strips. Using tongs, dip the whole husks into the water and blanch for about 10 seconds, or just until supple.

Chop the cactus into 1-inch cubes. You will need about ½ cup. Save any remainder for another use. Transfer the cubes to a nonreactive bowl, add the vinegar, and toss to coat. Let the cubes soak for about 20 minutes, then drain and rinse off the sticky residue. Set aside.

Lay 2 whole corn husks on a work surface, overlapping them by about ½ inch. Put a strip of fish lengthwise along the center of the husks. Put 3 or 4 cactus cubes,

1 teaspoon of the mayonnaise, a little of the onion, and 1 chile slice on either side of the fish. Lay 1 epazote leaf on top of the fish, and sprinkle the fish with a little paprika. Fold the long sides of the husks over, overlapping them by about ½ inch and closing the round bottom together snugly, then fold the top down to make a tight package. (The bottom is not folded because the round leaf base is not as supple.) Tie a strip of corn husk around the middle to close. Repeat with the remaining husks and ingredients to make 6 tamales.

Wrap each tamale in aluminum foil and place the packets in a small roasting pan. Pour water into the pan to a depth of about 1½ inches. Cover tightly with foil, place over medium heat, and bring to a boil. Immediately lower the heat to a simmer and steam for about 20 minutes, or until the fish is opaque and flakes easily (open a packet to check).

To serve, remove the foil from the tamales, and put the tamales on individual plates. Each diner unwraps the corn husks to reveal the filling.

COOK'S NOTE: *To remove the thorns from a cactus paddle, trim ½ inch off the stem end of the paddle. Then, using a gloved hand, hold the stem end and, with your other hand, slide a vegetable peeler across the surface, being careful to remove only the thorns and not the skin.*

A TYPICAL DISH found in many restaurants in Mexico City, these shrimp are a frequent item on our menu, too, often served with Saffron Rice (page 144) and Swiss chard. If you are having a party and serving an assortment of small dishes, this will fit right in. It is served piping hot in small, shallow terra-cotta dishes (*casuelitas*) and the accompanying warm tortillas are used to sop up any of the delicious sauce left in the dishes after the shrimp have been devoured. From start to finish, this takes less than an hour: about 20 minutes to prepare and 20 minutes to cook. Perfect!

sautéed shrimp in a fiery salsa

CASUELITA DE CAMARONES A LA DIABLA

SERVES 6

¼ cup olive oil

2 tablespoons finely chopped onion

1 tablespoon chopped garlic

3 pasilla chiles, seeded, membranes removed, and cut into ½-inch-thick rounds

3 ancho chiles, seeded, membranes removed, and cut into ½-inch-thick rounds

18 jumbo shrimp, peeled and deveined, with tail shell intact

Kosher salt and freshly ground black pepper

½ cup dry white wine

In a large skillet, heat the oil over medium-low heat. Add the onion and garlic and cook, stirring occasionally, for 2 to 3 minutes, or until tender but not browned.

Add the chiles and raise the heat to high. When the pan is hot, add the shrimp, season with salt and pepper, and cook, stirring and shaking the pan to ensure even cooking, for 3 to 4 minutes, or until they are pink but still translucent. Remove from the heat. Using a slotted spoon, transfer the shrimp to a plate or shallow bowl, leaving as much pan sauce as possible in the skillet.

Return the skillet to medium heat. Stir in the wine, simmer for about 30 seconds, then return the shrimp to the skillet. Raise the heat to high and bring to a boil. As soon as the liquid boils, remove the skillet from the heat.

Divide the shrimp and the pan juices evenly among 6 *casuelitas* or similar dishes. Serve piping hot.

IN MEXICO, seafood is frequently presented *al mojo de ajo*. Sometimes the *ajo*, or garlic, is crisped, and other times it is roasted, as we do here. Roasted garlic is mellow and sweet and tastes lovely with the shrimp. We know two meanings for the word *mojo*. In Spanish it means "to soak," and here the shrimp is soaked in garlic. In the African language of Yoruba, *mojo* means "soul," and this dish definitely has serious soul!

sautéed shrimp with golden garlic cloves

CASUELITA DE CAMARONES AL MOJO DE AJO

SERVES 6

3 heads garlic

About 1¼ cups olive oil

18 jumbo shrimp, peeled and deveined, with tail shell intact

2 tablespoons chopped fresh garlic

2 tablespoons chopped fresh flat-leaf parsley leaves

1 teaspoon kosher salt

Juice of 2 limes

6 sprigs flat-leaf parsley

Preheat the oven to 400°F. Remove the outer skins from the garlic heads, leaving the cloves attached. Slice off the top ½ inch from each head, and set each head in the center of a square of aluminum foil large enough to enclose it. Drizzle each head with a little of the oil, taking care to coat the whole head. Wrap the heads in their foil squares, enclosing loosely but completely.

Put the garlic packets on a rimmed baking sheet. Bake for about 30 minutes, or until the cloves feel soft when squeezed. Let the garlic cool in the foil.

Unwrap, remove 12 whole cloves, peel them, and set aside to use for garnish. Squeeze the remaining cloves from their skins into a blender. Add ¾ cup of the oil and process until smooth.

In a bowl, toss the shrimp with about ¼ cup of the garlic puree.

In a large nonstick skillet, heat 3 tablespoons of the oil over medium-high heat. (Or, to avoid crowding, use 2 skillets, with 3 tablespoons oil in each skillet.) Add the shrimp, chopped garlic, chopped parsley, and salt and cook, stirring, for 3 to 5 minutes, or until the shrimp curl, turn pink, and are opaque throughout. Stir ¼ cup of the garlic puree into the pan and continue to cook for 1 to 2 minutes. (Reserve the remaining garlic puree for another use. Store in a lidded container in the refrigerator for up to 5 days.)

Add the lime juice and cook, scraping up and dissolving any charred bits from the pan bottom, for about 30 seconds longer, or just until heated through.

Divide the shrimp evenly among 6 *casuelitas* (small, shallow terra-cotta dishes) or similar dishes. Garnish each serving with 2 whole roasted garlic cloves and 1 parsley sprig. Serve right away.

WE USE ONLY the chipotle-flavored adobo sauce, not the chipotle chile itself, for this dish because the chile's intensity would mask the saffron. Marrying those two flavors reflects the *mestizaje*, or cultural mixing, of Mexican cooking. The chipotle, a smoked jalapeño, dates from the pre-Columbian Aztec empire, and saffron arrived on tall ships with the conquistadors. These scallops and their sauce are also good served at room temperature.

sea scallops in a saffron and chipotle salsa

CALLOS A LA PLANCHA CON SALSA DE AZAFRÁN Y CHIPOTLE

SERVES 6

SCALLOPS
12 large sea scallops (about 1 pound)
Kosher salt and freshly ground black pepper
¼ to ½ cup all-purpose flour
¼ to ½ cup olive oil

SAUCE
2 tablespoons unsalted butter
2 tablespoons olive oil
1 shallot, minced (about 2 tablespoons)
2 tablespoons adobo from chipotles en adobo
½ cup dry white wine or fish stock
Pinch of saffron threads
⅛ teaspoon kosher salt

To prepare the scallops, using a paring knife or your fingers, remove and discard the small, tough membrane from the side of each scallop. Rinse the scallops and pat thoroughly dry. Season the scallops with salt and pepper.

Spread the flour on a flat plate. One at a time, roll each scallop in the flour, coating evenly and tapping off the excess.

In a large, heavy skillet, preferably cast iron, heat ¼ cup oil over high heat until a small cube of bread dropped into it sizzles on contact. (Or, to avoid crowding the scallops in the pan, use 2 skillets and heat ¼ cup oil in each pan.) Add the scallops and cook, without moving the scallops, for about 5 minutes, or until lightly crisped on the bottom and opaque about halfway up the sides. Turn the scallops over and cook for about 3 minutes longer, or until the bottoms are crisped and the sides are completely opaque. Reduce the heat to low and cook the scallops, without disturbing them, for 2 minutes longer. Transfer to a serving platter and cover loosely with aluminum foil to keep warm.

To make the sauce, in another heavy skillet, heat the butter and oil over medium-high heat until the butter melts. Lower the heat to medium, add the shallot, and cook, stirring occasionally, for 2 to 3 minutes, or until translucent. Do not allow to brown.

Stir in the adobo until combined, then whisk in the wine and bring to a boil. Boil for about 2 minutes, or until reduced by half. Add the saffron and salt and remove from the heat. Allow the sauce to rest for 2 minutes to infuse with the saffron.

Drizzle the sauce over the scallops and serve immediately.

A *PIPIÁN* IS A MOLE made with pumpkin seeds (*pepitas*). Here, the chile of choice is jalapeños, which make the sauce a lovely green. This is a relatively mild *pipián* from the Yucatán, so if you want a spicier mole, add more chile. We also serve this luscious sauce, which is almost like a pumpkin seed pesto, with tamales.

corn masa boats with mahimahi in a yucatecan pumpkin seed sauce

CHALUPAS DE PESCADO EN PIPIÁN YUCATECO

MAKES 12 CHALUPAS; SERVES 6

- 1½ cups pepitas (pumpkin seeds)
- 2 jalapeño chiles, seeded and membranes removed
- 1 small onion, chopped
- 2 cloves garlic
- ½ bunch cilantro, thick stems discarded
- About 2 cups low-sodium chicken broth, fish stock, or bottled clam juice
- 3 tablespoons corn oil
- ½ cup heavy cream
- Kosher salt and freshly ground black pepper
- 1 pound mahimahi or other mild, white fish fillets
- 12 Chalupas (page 140)
- ¼ cup finely chopped fresh cilantro leaves

In a dry cast-iron or nonstick pan, spread the *pepitas* in a single layer and toast over medium heat, stirring to prevent scorching, for about 3 minutes, or until aromatic and the seeds begin to pop. Remove from the heat and reserve 2 tablespoons of the toasted seeds for garnish.

In a blender or a food processor, combine the remaining *pepitas*, the chiles, onion, garlic, and the ½ bunch cilantro. With the motor running, slowly add enough of the broth—if you add it too quickly, the seeds won't

grind up completely—to form a smooth paste with the consistency of heavy cream.

In a saucepan, heat 2 tablespoons of the oil over medium heat. Transfer the pumpkin seed paste to the pan and cook, stirring occasionally, for about 5 minutes, or until the onion is cooked.

Reduce the heat to medium-low, add the cream, and bring to a simmer. Cook, stirring constantly, for about 5 minutes, or until the cream is heated through and the sauce is a uniform pale green and the consistency of heavy cream. Season with salt and pepper. Remove from the heat, cover, and set aside.

In a nonstick skillet, heat the remaining 1 tablespoon oil over medium-high heat. Add the fish and sear for about 3 minutes on each side, or until it is cooked through and flakes easily when prodded with a fork. Remove the fish from the pan and flake into 1-inch pieces. Season with salt and pepper.

Warm the *chalupas* as directed and arrange on a platter. Spoon a teaspoon of the pumpkin seed sauce into the center of each little boat. Top them evenly with the fish and more sauce. (You will have sauce left over. It will keep in a tightly covered container in the refrigerator for up to 5 days.) Sprinkle the *chalupas* and the platter with the reserved pumpkin seeds and the chopped cilantro. Serve right away.

MESTIZAJE: THE MIXING OF CULTURES

In Mexico City's aptly named Plaza de Tres Culturas, you will find an Aztec pyramid, a Catholic church that dates from the days of Spanish colonial rule, and a modern skyscraper. Mexican culture is a mixture of these three elements and more, including the United States (due to proximity), France (because Napoléon Bonaparte ruled Mexico), England, modern Spain, Asia, and Africa.

When Hernán Cortés landed near present-day Veracruz on the Gulf of Mexico in 1519, he found indigenous people who already had highly developed societies with wonderful art, architecture, and food—a rich heritage that has helped shape the complexity of the country's table. At the same time, Mexico has influenced gastronomy far beyond its borders, contributing such native foodstuffs as chocolate, vanilla, chiles, and corn to pantries around the world.

EVERYONE SEEMS TO LIKE *calamares fritos*, especially kids, whose faces light up when this dish is put on the table. The trick to making it is to have the calamari ready to fry before you begin to heat the oil. We serve fried calamari with our *cascabel* chile and tomatillo salsa, but this dish is also good with Avocado-Tomatillo Salsa (page 28) or Árbol Chile and Roasted Tomato Salsa (page 34).

fried calamari with cascabel chile salsa
CALAMARES FRITOS CON SALSA MACHA DE CASCABEL

SERVES 6

- 2½ pounds cleaned calamari (squid) bodies or mixture of bodies and tentacles
- 3 large eggs
- 1 cup fine-grind yellow cornmeal
- 1 teaspoon kosher salt
- 1 teaspoon piquín chile powder
- 1 teaspoon ancho chile powder
- 1 teaspoon sweet Spanish paprika
- Corn oil, for deep-frying
- Lime halves or wedges
- Rustic Cascabel Chile and Tomatillo Salsa (page 32)

Cut the calamari bodies into ½-inch-wide rings. Place in a bowl with the tentacles, add cold water to cover by 1 inch, and let stand for 30 minutes. Drain and spread on clean kitchen towels to dry.

In a bowl, beat the eggs until blended. In another bowl, whisk together the cornmeal, salt, both chile powders, and the paprika. Spread the cornmeal mixture on a large, flat plate or tray.

Drop 6 to 8 calamari pieces into the egg. Then, using a slotted spoon, lift them from the egg, draining them well over the bowl, and drop them into the cornmeal mixture. Toss to coat well, making sure the insides of the rings and the tentacles are coated evenly. Transfer the calamari pieces to a large sieve or a colander and shake once or twice to remove the excess cornmeal. Repeat until all the pieces are coated.

In a deep sauté pan or a large, wide pot, such as a Dutch oven, pour the oil to a depth of 3 inches and heat over medium-high heat to 375°F on a deep-frying thermometer, or until a piece of calamari dropped into the oil sizzles and turns golden in about 1 minute. Working in small batches, fry the calamari for about 2 minutes, or until evenly browned. Using a slotted spoon, transfer to paper towels to drain briefly. Let the oil return to temperature between batches.

Arrange the calamari on a warmed platter, garnish with the lime slices, and serve immediately with the salsa for dipping.

EL PAJARO

4 *aves*
POULTRY

THE POZOLE AT LA PALAPA is based on one of Barbara's mother's recipes. She is an artist living in Mexico City, and she often travels to the state of Jalisco to exhibit her paintings in Ajijic, an artists' colony, which is where she first ate this wonderful ancho chile–laced *pozole rojo*. It is an unusual pozole because most versions call for chile powder and add it at the end of cooking. Here, whole anchos are pureed and added earlier, so they infuse the dish more fully with their flavor and impart a rich color. We often serve this soup in espresso cups with demitasse spoons for parties. It also makes an easy and terrific main course for a family meal.

chicken and hominy soup

POZOLE ROJO

SERVES 6 TO 8 AS A FIRST COURSE, OR 4 TO 6 AS A MAIN COURSE

- 3 ancho chiles, seeded and membranes removed
- 2 cups water
- ½ cup coarsely chopped onion
- ½ cup coarsely chopped tomato
- ¼ cup corn oil
- 1 tablespoon crushed garlic
- 6 cups low-sodium chicken broth
- 2 cups ½-inch-cubed cooked chicken (see Chicken for Stuffing, page 145)
- 1 (15-ounce) can hominy, rinsed and drained
- ¼ teaspoon ground cumin
- Kosher salt

GARNISHES

- ½ cup chopped radishes
- 2 tablespoons dried Mexican oregano
- 2 teaspoons piquín chile powder
- 1 cup chopped avocado
- 1 cup shredded romaine lettuce
- Lime slices

In a small saucepan, combine the chiles and water and bring to a brisk simmer over medium-high heat. Lower the heat and simmer gently for about 15 minutes, or until softened. Drain the chiles, reserving the water. Transfer the chiles to a blender or food processor, add the onion and tomato, and process until smooth, adding the reserved water as needed to achieve a smooth consistency. Discard the remaining water.

In a skillet, heat the oil over medium heat. Add the garlic and cook for about 1 minute, or until it softens. Do not overcook. Add the tomato-chile paste (take care, as it will spatter) and cook, stirring occasionally, for about 5 minutes, or until cooked through and the oil rises to the top. Remove from the heat.

In a small stockpot, combine the broth, tomato-chile paste, and chicken and bring to a boil over medium-high heat. Add the hominy, return to a boil, and cook until heated through. Add the cumin and about 1 teaspoon salt, then taste and add more salt if needed. If the soup seems too thick, thin with a little water.

Ladle the soup into 4-ounce ramekins, espresso cups, or similar dishes for a first course, or into regular-size bowls for a main course. Top with as many of the garnishes as desired and serve immediately.

MARGARITTE ESPECIALLY LIKES the way the spicy chicken filling in these tacos is offset by the pickled red onions of the salsa. We first tasted this combination on Isla Mujeres, near Cancún, where the unspoiled beaches and slow pace combine for the perfect vacation. And nothing ends a restful day near the water like one of these tacos with a cold beer. Serve them family-style the next time you entertain a large, casual group.

roast achiote-rubbed chicken tacos

TACOS DE POLLO ROSTIZADO AL ACHIOTE

MAKES 12 TACOS; SERVES 6

MARINADE

2 guajillo chiles, seeded and membranes removed

1 árbol chile, seeded and membranes removed

1 cup freshly squeezed orange juice (about 3 oranges)

¼ cup olive oil

¼ cup achiote paste

2 tablespoons honey

½ teaspoon ground cumin

1 teaspoon kosher salt

1 (3½-pound) chicken, rinsed and patted dry

Kosher salt and freshly ground black pepper

12 (6-inch) corn tortillas

½ cup chopped fresh cilantro leaves

1 avocado, halved, pitted, peeled, and sliced

1 cup Pickled Red Onion and Habanero Chile Salsa (page 36)

To make the marinade, put the chiles in a nonreactive bowl, add hot water to cover, and let stand for about 20 minutes to soften, then drain. Transfer the chiles to a blender, add the orange juice, oil, achiote paste, honey, cumin, and salt, and process until liquefied.

Season the chicken, inside and out, with salt and pepper. Transfer to a nonreactive bowl large enough to hold it comfortably, and pour all but ¼ cup of the marinade over it. Be sure to get some of the marinade inside the cavity. Cover and refrigerate for at least 6 hours or up to 12 hours.

Preheat the oven to 400°F. Lift the chicken from the marinade, letting the excess drip back into the bowl. Reserve the marinade. Put the chicken in a nonstick roasting pan.

Roast the chicken for about 20 minutes to crisp the skin. Baste with about 2 tablespoons of the marinade and continue roasting for about 20 minutes. Baste the chicken one more time with some of the marinade (discard the remaining marinade), then tent with aluminum foil so the skin does not scorch. Roast for about 40 minutes longer, or until the juices run clear when a thigh joint is pierced with a knife tip.

Transfer the chicken to a cutting board and let rest for about 15 minutes. Meanwhile, warm the tortillas (see page 130).

Remove the legs, thighs, and wings from the chicken. Remove the meat from the thighs, legs, and breast and slice it. (Reserve the wings and back for another use.) Cut twelve 6-inch squares of parchment paper. Lay a tortilla on a parchment square. Put about 2 tablespoons chicken down the center, and top with some of the cilantro and avocado. Using the parchment, fold the tortilla in half and transfer to a serving plate. Repeat until all the ingredients are used, then arrange the tacos side by side on the plate so that they hold one another up. Serve the salsa on the side.

CINE DE ORO

At La Palapa, we serve authentic Mexican food, but we also strive to share Mexican art and culture with the New Yorkers who make up most of our customer base. At our restaurant in Greenwich Village, we display art dedicated to the Golden Age of Mexican cinema (late 1930s to late 1950s), during which hundreds of Spanish-language films were made in Mexico City. When Senator Joseph McCarthy's national anticommunist campaign prompted the creation of a Hollywood blacklist in the late 1940s, many of the American film actors, directors, writers, and cinematographers it targeted found a home and an artistic outlet south of the border.

Photographs by famed cinematographer Gabriel Figueroa also adorn the restaurant walls. We met Figueroa's son, Gabo, a photographer as well, in Mexico City and toured his studio, then convinced him to print photos of golden-era icon María Félix, "La Doña," from his father's archives. He also printed a magnificent colorized photo of another icon of the time, Pedro Armendáriz, astride his horse. And finally, a photo mural of Rosa Carmina and her Rumbera Girls hangs over the bar. Born in Cuba in 1929, she was a golden-age cinema star, famous for her exotic dances. We once joined her for lunch at her home in Mexico City, and after a mouthwatering Cuban-Mexican meal, she dedicated the photo to us.

ENCASING FOOD IN LEAVES for cooking is a time-honored Mexican tradition, and one that reportedly pleased Cuauhtémoc, the last Aztec emperor. Whether the cook uses corn husks, banana leaves, or *hoja santa* leaves for wrapping, the flavors of the chiles, spices, and fruits percolating inside intensify gloriously. This full-flavored yet mild dish is typical of the cooking of the Yucatán.

guajillo chile–rubbed chicken wrapped in banana leaves

POLLITOS EN MIXIOTES YUCATECOS

SERVES 6

CHILE RUB

4 guajillo chiles, seeded and membranes removed

1 árbol chile, seeded and membranes removed

1 cup freshly squeezed orange juice (about 3 oranges)

¼ cup chopped white onion

4 cloves garlic, coarsely chopped

Kosher salt

½ teaspoon ground cloves

½ teaspoon ground cumin

½ teaspoon freshly ground black pepper

½ teaspoon dried Mexican oregano

½ teaspoon dried thyme

¼ cup achiote paste

2 tablespoons freshly squeezed lime juice

2 tablespoons orange-flavored liqueur, such as triple sec

1 tablespoon honey

1 fresh or dried avocado leaf or bay leaf

6 bone-in chicken thighs, rinsed, patted dry, and skinned

Kosher salt and freshly ground black pepper

6 (10- to 12-inch) squares banana leaf, plus 6 banana leaf strips for tying (see Cook's Note)

About 2 tablespoons corn oil, or vegetable oil spray

12 slices onion

12 slices plum tomato

Saffron Rice (page 144)

Pickled Red Onion and Habanero Chile Salsa (page 36)

Tortillas, warmed (see page 130), for serving

To make the chile rub, place the chiles in a bowl, add hot water to cover, and let stand for 20 minutes to soften, then drain. In a food processor or blender, combine the orange juice, onion, and garlic and process until liquefied. Add the chiles and pulse to mix. Add 2 teaspoons salt, the cloves, cumin, pepper, oregano, and thyme and process until smooth. Add the achiote paste, lime juice, liqueur, and honey and process again until smooth. Taste and adjust the salt, if needed. It should be pleasantly salty. Transfer to a large, nonreactive bowl and add the avocado leaf.

Season the thighs on all sides with salt and pepper. Transfer the thighs to the rub and turn to coat evenly. Cover and refrigerate for at least 6 hours or up to 12 hours.

CONTINUED ▶

Preheat the oven to 375°F. Place the banana leaf squares, vein side up, on a work surface, and coat lightly with the oil. Put a thigh and 3 tablespoons of the rub on the center of a square, and top with 2 onion slices and 2 tomato slices. Fold the left and right sides in, overlapping them, then fold down the top and fold up the bottom, to form a square parcel. Tie a banana leaf strip around the parcel, and then wrap the parcel in aluminum foil, sealing well. Repeat to make 6 parcels total.

Put the parcels in a deep roasting pan. Pour water to a depth of about 1 inch into the pan and cover tightly with foil. Bake for 1¼ hours, or until the chicken is cooked through (open a parcel to check).

Discard the foil and and place the parcels on individual plates. Each diner unwraps the leaf to reveal the filling. Serve with the rice, salsa, and tortillas.

COOK'S NOTE: *Banana leaves are sold both fresh and frozen in Latin and Southeast Asian stores. If purchased frozen, thaw at room temperature. Rinse the fresh or thawed leaves and wipe dry to remove any residue. Bring a large pot filled with water to a boil. One at a time, blanch the leaves for about 15 seconds to soften, then drain, dry, and cut into the size needed. A leaf's veins can make folding difficult, so trim off any veins on the edges.*

WE LEARNED THIS RECIPE from our friend Paulina Barrera, who made hundreds of tamales a day for a *tamalera*, a woman who sells tamales door-to-door. The beauty of this method is that the *masa* is cooked before the corn husks are stuffed with it. Then, when the tamales are steamed, the *masa* cooks a second time, ensuring a delicious result. This recipe yields 24 tamales, but the extras can be well wrapped and frozen for up to 1 month.

chicken tamales with cooked tomatillo salsa

TAMALES DE POLLO VERDES

MAKES 24 TAMALES; SERVES 12

30 corn husks (see Cook's Note)

2 cups masa harina for tamales (see Cook's Note)

1 cup high-quality lard, at room temperature

1 teaspoon kosher salt

7 cups tepid water

3 cups Cooked Tomatillo Salsa (page 34)

1½ cups shredded cooked chicken (see Chicken for Stuffing, page 145)

Put the corn husks in a shallow dish, add hot water to cover, and let soak for 1 hour. Drain and rinse to remove any silk. Cover the husks with a damp kitchen towel and set aside.

While the husks are soaking, in a small stockpot, use your hands to mix together the *masa harina*, lard, and salt. Add the water and mix with your hands or a wooden spoon until the mixture is smooth and the consistency of heavy cream.

Put the pot over medium-low heat and cook, stirring constantly, for about 20 minutes, or until the *masa* is no longer lumpy and is shiny and almost translucent. Remove from the heat and cover.

Tear 1 husk lengthwise into strips about ¼ inch wide. To shape each tamale, put a corn husk in the palm of your hand. The base, or "navel," of the leaf should reach your wrist. Place in the hollow of the husk, in the following order, 1 tablespoon salsa, 2 tablespoons *masa*, 1 tablespoon salsa, and 1 tablespoon shredded chicken. Loosely (so there is room to expand) fold the sides of the corn husk into the center, overlapping them slightly. Fold the narrow end of the husk over the seam, then fold the broad end of the husk over the top. Tie a husk strip loosely around the center. Repeat to make 24 tamales total. (You may have *masa* left over.)

Pour water into the bottom of a large steamer, and put the steamer tray in place. Make sure the water does not touch the bottom of the tray. Stand the tamales vertically in the steamer, with the "navel" end facing upward. (If the tamales will not fit without crowding, steam in 2 batches or 2 steamers.) Lay plastic wrap over the tamales (it helps form a tight seal), and then cover the steamer tightly.

Bring the water to a boil, reduce the heat to low, and simmer for about 1 hour. Check the pan occasionally and add more boiling water if the water threatens to boil away. To test for doneness, remove 1 tamale from the center of the rack and unwrap the husk.

CONTINUED ▸

If the dough pulls away easily and is firm and smooth, the tamales are ready.

To serve, lay 1 or 2 tamales on each plate and serve at once. Let diners unwrap their own tamales at the table.

COOK'S NOTE: *The best corn husks are thin and flexible, with an intact "navel," or circle, where the leaf was attached to the ear. We need only 25 husks for the tamales and ties, but the husks tear easily, so it is good to have extras on hand. Buy Maseca brand* masa harina *for tamales (Maseca is the most common brand of* masa harina*), which is more coarsely ground than the regular* masa harina *used for tortillas. If you cannot find it, the latter can be used.*

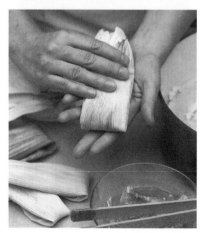

THESE SWEET-AND-SAVORY TOSTADAS are great favorites at the weddings and other large parties we cater. The smoky chipotle-fig sauce has become a La Palapa specialty that nicely complements the slightly gamy flavor of duck.

duck breast tostadas with chipotle-fig sauce
TOSTADAS DE PATO CON SALSA DE HIGO Y CHIPOTLE

MAKES 36 TOSTADAS; SERVES 8 TO 12

SAUCE

1 cup dried figs (about 10), such as Mission, halved lengthwise

1 cup firmly packed light or dark brown sugar

3 chipotles en adobo

1 tablespoon adobo from chipotles en adobo

Kosher salt

6 (6-inch) blue or white corn tortillas

1 cup corn oil

Kosher salt

2 cups sliced cooked duck (see Grilled Duck, page 145), at room temperature

3 tablespoons chopped fresh cilantro leaves

3 tablespoons crumbled queso fresco or ricotta salata cheese

To make the sauce, put the figs in a bowl, add warm water to cover, and set aside for about 20 minutes to soften. Drain and reserve the soaking water.

Transfer the figs to a blender or food processor, add the brown sugar, chipotles, and adobo, and process until smooth. Add as much of the soaking water as needed to create a syrupy consistency. Season to taste with salt.

To make the tostadas, using a cookie cutter, cut the tortillas into 2-inch rounds. Or, using a knife, cut each tortilla into 6 wedges.

In a deep sauté pan, heat the oil over medium-high heat until a small piece of tortilla dropped into the oil crisps within 15 seconds. Fry the tortilla pieces, a few at a time, for about 15 seconds on the first side, or until they start to curl. Turn and fry on the second side for 15 seconds. Be careful not to overcook. Using a slotted spoon, transfer to paper towels to drain. Let the oil regain temperature between batches.

Spread the hot tostadas on a platter and season with salt. Top each tostada with some of the duck, drizzle with a little of the sauce, and sprinkle with the cilantro and cheese. Serve at once.

THESE CRISP, ROLLED TORTILLAS, or *taquitos*, are named for the town of Puebla, the site of the Battle of Puebla, in which local forces defeated the occupying French army on May 5, 1862—a victory marked today by the national celebration of Cinco de Mayo. Serve them on a platter accompanied by red salsa, white *crema*, and green guacamole—the colors of the Mexican flag.

crisp tortillas stuffed with puebla-style chipotle chicken and potato

TAQUITOS DE TINGA POBLANA Y PAPA

MAKES 24 TAQUITOS; SERVES 6 TO 8

- 6 plum tomatoes, cored and quartered
- 2 chipotles en adobo with most of the adobo wiped off
- ¼ cup chopped onion
- 1 clove garlic
- ¼ teaspoon ground cumin
- ¼ teaspoon freshly ground white pepper
- 3 tablespoons corn oil
- 3 cups shredded cooked chicken (see Chicken for Stuffing, page 145)

POTATOES

- 3 russet potatoes, peeled and cut into large chunks
- 1 large egg, beaten
- ½ cup grated queso Cotija or Parmesan cheese
- 1 tablespoon chopped epazote leaves
- 2 teaspoons kosher salt
- 1 teaspoon chopped jalapeño chile
- 24 (4- or 6-inch) corn tortillas

Corn oil, for deep-frying
1 cup Árbol Chile and Roasted Tomato Salsa (page 24)
1 cup Crema Mexicana (page 139)
1 cup La Palapa's Classic Guacamole (page 14)

In a blender, combine the tomatoes, chiles, onion, garlic, cumin, and pepper and process until liquefied.

In a deep sauté pan, heat the oil over medium-low heat. Add the tomato mixture and cook, stirring constantly, for about 20 minutes, or until it turns a deep, dark red, the oil is incorporated, and the mixture has reduced by about one-third. Fold in the chicken and simmer for about 10 minutes, or until heated through and evenly covered with the sauce. Remove from the heat.

Meanwhile, cook the potatoes. In a saucepan, combine the potatoes with water to cover, bring to a boil, and boil for about 20 minutes, or until fork-tender. Drain and return to the pot. Using a fork or potato masher, mash the potatoes until nearly smooth. Let cool in the pan.

CONTINUED ▶

Add the egg, cheese, epazote, salt, and chile to the cooled potatoes and mix well. Squeeze as much moisture as possible from 1 cup of the chicken mixture and place in a bowl. Fold in 1 cup of the potato mixture. Reserve the remaining chicken and potato mixtures for another use. They will keep, tightly covered, in the refrigerator for up to 5 days.

Warm the tortillas (see page 130), and wrap them in a kitchen towel to keep them warm and supple.

Spoon a heaping tablespoon of the filling down the center of a tortilla, roll it up tightly around the filling, and spear it onto a 6-inch wooden skewer. Repeat to fill 2 more tortillas and add them to the skewer. Then, repeat with the remaining tortillas and filling, to fill 8 skewers total.

In a deep sauté pan, pour the oil to a depth of 2 inches and heat over medium-high heat to 350°F on a deep-frying thermometer, or until a small piece of tortilla dropped into the oil sizzles on contact. Working in batches, add the skewers and deep-fry for about 5 minutes, or until the tortillas are crisp and evenly golden brown. Using a slotted spoon or tongs, transfer to paper towels to drain. Scoop out any filling that escapes from the tortillas into the oil, and let the oil return to temperature between batches.

When all of the skewers are cooked, arrange them on a platter and serve at once, accompanied with the salsa, *crema*, and guacamole.

ONE OF THESE *SOPES* is a delicious *antojito* or snack. A plate with three or four is a feast! We like to make them with pan-grilled and sliced duck breast, but shredded roasted duck meat is just as tasty. Or, you can substitute beef, chicken, or pork. We have also made this dish with sweet plantains topped with the mole for a spectacular vegetarian option.

fresh tortillas with duck in oaxaca-style black mole

SOPES DE PATO EN MOLE NEGRO

MAKES 16 SMALL SOPES; SERVES 8

1¼ cups masa harina

½ teaspoon kosher salt

1 cup plus 2 tablespoons warm water

Corn oil, for deep-frying and for cooking the sopes

2 cups Oaxaca-Style Black Mole (page 142)

2 cups sliced cooked duck (see page 145), at room temperature

½ cup crumbled queso fresco or ricotta salata cheese

½ cup Crema Mexicana (page 139)

¼ cup sesame seeds, toasted

In a bowl, whisk together the *masa harina* and salt. Make a well in the center, add the 1 cup warm water, and knead with your hands until the mixture comes together in a dough and forms a ball. If the dough feels too dry, add as much of the remaining 2 tablespoons water as needed.

Divide the dough into 16 equal pieces. Keep them covered with plastic wrap when you are not working with them. Roll each piece between your palms into a small, flattened ball about 2 inches in diameter. Place on a work surface, cover with plastic wrap, and press down until the dough is about 4 inches in diameter and ¼ inch thick.

In a heavy sauté pan, pour the oil to a depth of about 2 inches and heat over medium-high heat to 375°F on a deep-frying thermometer, or until a small piece of dough dropped into the oil sizzles on contact. Working in batches, add the dough rounds and fry, turning once, for about 2 minutes on each side, or until lightly crispy on the outside and soft on the inside. Using a slotted spoon, transfer to paper towels to drain. Let the oil regain temperature between batches.

When the rounds are cool enough to handle, after about 3 minutes, use your thumb and index finger to form a ½-inch rim around the edge, creating a boat shape. Pinch up the thick center to form a thinner, craggy "crater" for holding the sauce and filling. These tiny center ridges will help anchor the filling and ensure the dough cooks through. (If not serving right away, let cool and store in a lidded container in the refrigerator for up to 3 days.)

While the *sopes* are cooking, in the top of a double boiler over gently simmering water, warm the mole, stirring often.

Lightly oil a nonstick skillet and place over medium heat. Working in batches, arrange the *sopes*, hollow side up, in a single layer and brush each with a little oil.

CONTINUED ▸

Warm for about 2 minutes. Turn the *sopes* over to warm the other side. This final cooking also ensures the center is cooked through.

With the hollow side up, spoon about 1 tablespoon mole into each "boat" and cover with duck. Leave the *sopes* in the skillet for a minute or two to continue to warm. Transfer to warmed individual plates, and repeat with the rest of the *sopes*.

Drizzle the *sopes* with more mole, and top with the cheese and *crema*. Garnish with a sprinkling of sesame seeds and serve at once.

SOPES

Made from thick, handmade tortillas, these small oval shells—about 4 inches across—have pinched centers and small rims, the ideal size and shape for cradling rich *mole negro* or other flavorful fillings for eating out of hand. *Sopes* are sold in outdoor markets across Mexico, where they are the perfect snack to munch as you amble through the narrow stalls and wide plazas. The best ones, which are usually quickly cooked on a griddle or skillet, are crispy on the bottom and soft on the top and are generously piled with bright, fresh, spicy ingredients.

When we are in Mexico, we head to the corn mill, or *molino de nixtamal*, for freshly milled *masa harina* for making *sopes*. Back home in New York, we have to rely on store-bought flour, which is available in most supermarkets.

Año Nuevo | NEW YEAR'S DAY

In Mexico, New Year's Day is a time of dancing and fiestas. January 1 is one of our busiest days at La Palapa, and we celebrate it with an all-day brunch menu we call *Menu de la Cruda*, or Hangover Specials of the Day. The fiery *michelada*, a delicious beer cocktail, or homemade *sangrita* with a shot of tequila are good choices for the day. If you want to serve your favorite Bloody Mary, rim the glass with Piquín Chile Salt (page 138), add some tequila, and you have a Bloody Maria! Be sure to offer a good selection of salsas, including a spicy serrano salsa, a mild tomatillo salsa, and a creamy árbol chile salsa with the dishes. And don't forget to serve a basket of warm tortillas. At the end of the meal, we offer our famous three-milk cake—a delicious way to start the new year!

SERVES 12

chelada y michelada
MEXICAN BEER COCKTAILS (PAGE 11)

tequila y sangrita
TEQUILA WITH SANGRITA (PAGE 9)

cacahuates enchilados
SPICY ROASTED PEANUTS (PAGE 18)

salsa de chile serrano torreado
CHARRED SERRANO CHILE SALSA (PAGE 22)

guacasalsa
AVOCADO-TOMATILLO SALSA (PAGE 28)

salsa de cacahuate y chile de árbol
PEANUT AND ÁRBOL CHILE SALSA (PAGE 35)

pozole rojo
CHICKEN AND HOMINY SOUP (PAGE 60)

pollitos en mixiotes yucatecos
GUAJILLO CHILE–RUBBED CHICKEN WRAPPED IN BANANA LEAVES (PAGE 65)

queso fundido de esquites
BAKED CORN WITH EPAZOTE AND CHEESE (PAGE 119)

arrachera al tequila
TEQUILA-AND-LIME-MARINATED SKIRT STEAK (PAGE 84)

cebollitas asadas
GRILLED SPRING ONIONS WITH SEA SALT AND LIME (PAGE 126)

frijoles pintos tradicionales
SLOW-COOKED VEGETARIAN PINTO BEANS (PAGE 146)

pastel tres leches de la palapa
LA PALAPA'S THREE-MILK CAKE (PAGE 77)

AS A CHILD, BARBARA REMEMBERS visiting the home of family friend Elsie Escobedo, where she was encouraged to indulge in thick slices of Doña Nico's wonderful *pastel tres leches*. Artists such as Leonora Carrington and Helen Escobedo would also gather to enjoy this delectable cake and sip strong black tea.

At La Palapa, the moist, light-textured cake is served in tall slices that have been described as looking like a "delicious cruise ship" floating on a sea of the "*tres leches*"! We pile the meringue frosting high, twirled into whimsical peaks, and at the last minute, we drizzle the yellow cake with the intoxicating combination of three milks.

la palapa's three-milk cake

PASTEL TRES LECHES DE LA PALAPA

MAKES 1 (9-INCH) CAKE; SERVES 12

CAKE

2½ cups all-purpose flour

1 teaspoon baking powder

8 large eggs, separated

1¼ cups sugar

¾ cup whole milk

1½ teaspoons pure vanilla extract, preferably Mexican

1 (12-ounce) can evaporated milk

1 (14-ounce) can sweetened condensed milk

1 cup heavy cream

FROSTING

8 large egg whites, or 1 cup frozen egg whites, thawed

¼ teaspoon cream of tartar

Pinch of kosher salt

¾ cup water

1½ cups sugar

TRES LECHES

1 (12-ounce) can evaporated milk

1 (14-ounce) can sweetened condensed milk

1 cup heavy cream

Zest of 1 lime, in thin strips

To make the cake, preheat the oven to 375°F. Butter a 9-inch springform pan, dust with flour, and tap out the excess.

In a bowl, sift together the flour and baking powder and set aside.

Using a stand mixer fitted with the whisk attachment, whip the egg whites on high speed until foamy. While continuing to whip, gradually add the sugar. When all of the sugar has been added and the egg whites have formed soft peaks, begin adding the egg yolks, one at a time, beating after each addition until incorporated. Continue beating until billowy.

CONTINUED ▶

On medium speed, add the flour mixture in ½-cup additions alternately with the whole milk in about ¼-cup additions, beginning and ending with the flour mixture and beating after each addition until combined. Finally, add the vanilla and mix gently for about 20 seconds. Do not rush this step or the cake will bake unevenly.

Pour the batter into the prepared pan. Bake for about 40 minutes, or until a toothpick inserted into the center comes out clean. Let cool in the pan on a wire rack for 20 minutes, then unclasp and carefully lift off the pan sides. Slide the cake off the pan bottom onto the rack and let cool completely.

Using a serrated knife, cut the cooled cake horizontally into 2 layers. Put each layer on a plate. (If the top of the cake domed a bit during baking, and you prefer a flat-topped cake for frosting, carefully slice off the domed top.)

In a nonreactive bowl, combine the evaporated milk, condensed milk, and cream and set aside.

To make the frosting, using the stand mixer fitted with the whisk attachment, whip the egg whites, cream of tartar, and salt on high speed until stiff peaks form. Set aside.

In a saucepan, combine the water and sugar and bring to a boil over medium-high heat, stirring until the sugar dissolves. Continue to boil, without stirring, until the mixture registers 234° to 240°F on a candy thermometer (soft ball stage), or until a tiny bit of syrup dropped into a small bowl of cold water forms a soft, flexible ball when pressed between your fingertips.

With the mixer on low speed, slowly add the syrup to the egg whites, aiming it between the whisk and the bowl sides to avoid spatters. When all of the syrup has been incorporated, increase the speed to medium-high and beat for about 5 minutes, or until stiff, firm peaks form. The frosting will be glossy and firm.

Slowly pour the reserved milk mixture over the 2 cake layers, dividing it evenly. The cake will soak up most of the mixture and some will begin to seep out—delicious!

Carefully transfer the moistened bottom layer to a cake plate or cake stand. Top with one-fourth of the frosting, spreading it evenly over the cake layer. Set the second cake layer on top, and frost the top and sides of the cake with the remaining frosting, creating swirls on top.

To make the *tres leches*, in a nonreactive bowl, stir together the evaporated milk, condensed milk, and cream and set aside.

To serve, gently score the cake into the number of slices needed by marking the frosting with a long knife blade (not serrated). (The best way to ensure even slices is first to score the cake into halves and then into quarters, and then each quarter into thirds.) Slice the cake gently, wiping the knife blade clean with a damp cloth after each slice.

For each serving, drizzle the center of an individual serving plate with 2 tablespoons of the *tres leches*, forming a pool. Stand a cake slice upright on the pool, and drizzle the slice with 2 tablespoons of *tres leches*. Garnish with a few strips of lime zest. Pass the remaining *tres leches* at the table for guests to drizzle as desired.

LA CHALUPA

5 *carnes*
BEEF, LAMB, AND PORK

empanadas de picadillo en nogada
**BEEF EMPANADAS WITH
WALNUT CREMA** | 82

arrachera al tequila
**TEQUILA-AND-LIME-
MARINATED SKIRT
STEAK** | 84

*tacos de barbacaoa de cordero
en chile ancho de catalina*
**ANCHO CHILE–BRAISED
LAMB TACOS** | 86

*albóndigas al chipotle
con guacasalsa*
**MEATBALLS IN CHIPOTLE
CHILE WITH AVOCADO-
TOMATILLO SALSA** | 88

chalupas con chorizo
**CORN MASA BOATS
WITH CHORIZO** | 90

FIESTA MENU:
CUMPLEAÑOS | 93

tacos de puerco rostizado
ROAST PORK TACOS | 94

costillitas al adobo de chile mulato
**PORK RIBS IN A MULATO
CHILE ADOBO** | 97

queso fundido con chorizo
**CHEESE BAKED WITH
GUAJILLO-SPIKED
CHORIZO** | 99

*tortas de jamón serrano y queso
chihuahua en panecillo de elote*
**SERRANO HAM,
CHEESE, AND AVOCADO
SANDWICH ON POBLANO
CORN BREAD** | 100

THIS *ANTOJITO* IS ANOTHER EXAMPLE of the varied influences on Mexican cuisine. The town of Pachuca, which lies about ninety miles north of Mexico City, has long been a center for silver mining, and in the early 1800s, miners from Cornwall, England, settled there. They brought with them the tradition of pasties, which are knowns as *pastes* in Pachuca and as empanadas in other parts of Mexico.

At La Palapa, we fill our empanadas with a beef *picadillo* that is reminiscent of the stuffing for *chiles en nogada*, thus the garnish of *crema de nogada* (walnut *crema*).

beef empanadas with walnut crema
EMPANADAS DE PICADILLO EN NOGADA

MAKES 12 EMPANADAS; SERVES 6

DOUGH
2¼ cups all-purpose flour

½ cup (1 stick) cold unsalted butter, cut into cubes

1½ teaspoons kosher salt

1 large egg, beaten

⅓ cup ice water

1 tablespoon distilled white vinegar

FILLING
3 tablespoons corn oil

1 onion, chopped

4 cloves garlic, chopped

2 poblano chiles, seeded, membranes removed, and chopped

4 plum tomatoes, chopped

½ cup chopped fresh cilantro leaves and thin stems

1 teaspoon dried thyme

⅛ teaspoon ground cloves

2 bay leaves

1 (3-inch) stick Mexican cinnamon

2 pounds ground beef

Kosher salt and freshly ground black pepper

½ cup diced, peeled apple

¼ cup chopped candied pineapple

¼ cup pine nuts

¼ cup slivered almonds

¼ cup raisins, soaked in sherry or warm water to soften

1 large egg yolk, lightly beaten

WALNUT CREMA
½ cup queso fresco or ricotta cheese

½ teaspoon kosher salt, if using ricotta cheese

½ cup walnut halves

1 cup Crema Mexicana (page 139)

3 tablespoons sherry

½ teaspoon sugar

About 12 sprigs flat-leaf parsley

½ cup pomegranate seeds

To make the dough, in a food processor, combine the flour, butter, and salt and pulse until the mixture resembles small peas. Transfer to a bowl and add the egg, water, and vinegar. Using your hands or a wooden spoon, or both, work the mixture until it holds together in a cohesive mass. Cover and refrigerate for about 20 minutes.

On a floured work surface, roll out the dough into a rectangle about ¼ inch thick. Using a 6-inch round template, cut out 12 rounds. If necessary, reroll the dough scraps and cut additional rounds. Cover the rounds with a barely damp kitchen towel.

To make the filling, in a large sauté pan, heat the oil over medium heat. Add the onion and garlic and sauté for about 3 minutes, or until the onion softens. Add the chiles, tomatoes, cilantro, thyme, cloves, bay leaves, and cinnamon stick and cook for about 3 minutes, or until the tomatoes release their juices. Add the beef and sauté, breaking it up with a wooden spoon, for about 5 minutes, or until cooked through. Season with salt and pepper. Add the apple, pineapple, pine nuts, almonds, and raisins and sauté for about 5 minutes longer, or until the apple softens. Taste and adjust with salt, if needed.

Preheat the oven to 375°F. Put about 2 tablespoons of the filling on half of a dough round, dampen the rim with water, and fold the round to form a half-moon.

Crimp the edges closed with fork tines, and make a small steam vent on the top side. Repeat to make 12 empanadas total. (You will have filling left over. Store in a tightly covered container in the refrigerator for up to 5 days, and use for tostadas, quesadillas, or chiles rellenos.)

Arrange the empanadas on a rimmed baking sheet. Brush the tops with the egg yolk. Bake for about 20 minutes, or until golden brown.

Meanwhile, make the *crema*. In a food processor or a blender, combine the cheese, salt, walnuts, *crema*, sherry, and sugar and process until smooth and creamy.

Transfer the empanadas to a platter and garnish with a dollop of the *crema*, a parsley sprig, and a sprinkle of pomegranate seeds. Serve right away.

THE MARINADE FOR THIS POPULAR LA PALAPA DISH was concocted one afternoon when we were grilling and making margaritas at the same time, and some of the ingredients for the cocktails made it into the marinade. We discovered the tasty, tender result when we sat down to eat the steaks. The meat is marinated just long enough to absorb the delicious smokiness of tequila and the fresh bite of the lime.

tequila-and-lime-marinated skirt steak

ARRACHERA AL TEQUILA

SERVES 6

2 pounds skirt steak, fat trimmed

1 cup olive oil

½ onion, sliced

½ cup tequila

Juice of 2 limes

1 tablespoon sugar

1 tablespoon kosher salt

1 teaspoon freshly ground black pepper

2 tablespoons corn oil

Grilled Spring Onions with Sea Salt and Lime (page 126)

1 cup Peanut and Árbol Chile Salsa (page 35)

Rinse the steak under cool water and pat dry with a paper towel.

In a nonreactive bowl or rigid plastic container with a tight-fitting lid, mix together the olive oil, onion, tequila, lime juice, sugar, salt, and pepper. Put the steak in the bowl and turn to coat. Cover and refrigerate for 30 minutes. Do not leave any longer or the lime juice will toughen the steak.

Heat the corn oil in a large, nonstick sauté pan over medium-high heat, or prepare a hot fire in a charcoal or gas grill. Before igniting the grill, lightly coat the grill grid with corn oil to prevent sticking.

Lift the steak from the marinade, letting most of the marinade drip back into the bowl, and place in the pan or on the grill grid. Cook, turning once, for about 2 minutes on each side, or until nicely seared and medium-rare. Test for doneness by pressing the thickest part of the steak with your finger. If it does not spring back at all, it is too rare.

Transfer the steak to a cutting board and let rest for about 10 minutes.

Slice the steak across the grain into ½-inch-wide strips. Arrange the slices on a serving platter and garnish the platter with the onions. Drizzle the steak with half of the salsa and serve. Pass the remaining salsa at the table.

WHEN BARBARA'S MOTHER, painter Kathleen Clement, first moved to Mexico City in the 1960s to become part of the vibrant expatriate community, she fell in love with this dish. When she could, she made it as the Mayans have made it for centuries. The technique, which is known as *barbacoa*, or "barbecue," calls for wrapping the meat in leaves and braising it in a leaf-lined *pib*, or pit. Traditionally, huge maguey leaves were used for both the wrapping and the lining, but they are not easy to find these days, even in Mexico, so we rely on ancho chiles for wrapping the lamb, with equally delicious results.

ancho chile–braised lamb tacos

TACOS DE BARBACOA DE CORDERO EN CHILE ANCHO DE CATALINA

MAKES 12 TACOS; SERVES 6

CHILE PASTE
22 ancho chiles
2 cups boiling water
6 cloves garlic
1 teaspoon kosher salt

LAMB
6 lamb shanks, about 1 pound each
Kosher salt and freshly ground black pepper
12 fresh or dried avocado leaves, or 6 fresh or dried bay leaves
3 tablespoons olive oil
4 cups low-sodium chicken broth or water

12 (6-inch) corn tortillas
1 cup La Palapa's Classic Guacamole (page 14)
12 sprigs cilantro

To make the chile paste, using a large, dry griddle, grill pan, or cast-iron skillet, toast the chiles over medium heat, turning them with tongs, for 20 to 30 seconds, or until lightly and evenly charred and fragrant. Transfer to a nonreactive bowl and add the boiling water. Set aside for 15 minutes, or until soft and limp.

Drain the chiles, reserving the soaking water. Slit 12 of the chiles lengthwise and remove the stems, seeds, and membranes, keeping each chile in one piece. Set the 12 chiles aside. Remove and discard the stems, seeds, and membranes from the remaining 10 chiles, and place in a blender.

Add 2 to 3 tablespoons of the reserved water and the garlic and process until smooth, adding more water if needed to achieve a smooth consistency. Add the salt and blend for 30 seconds longer.

To cook the lamb, preheat the oven to 325°F. Season the shanks on all sides with salt and pepper. Rub the chile paste evenly over the shanks. Lay 2 avocado leaves or 1 bay leaf on top of each shank. Wrap each shank with 2 of the reserved chiles, with the chiles skin side out.

Pour the oil into a roasting pan large enough to hold the shanks in a single layer, and place the shanks, meaty side down, in the pan. Pour the broth into the pan. The shanks should be nearly submerged. If they are not, add water as needed. Cover tightly with aluminum foil.

Braise the shanks in the oven for about 2½ hours, or until the meat is very tender and falls easily off the bone when prodded with a fork.

Transfer the shanks to a platter, spoon a little of the braising liquid over them, and then pull the meat from the bones. Reserve the remaining braising liquid.

Warm the tortillas (see page 130). Cut twelve 6-inch squares of parchment paper. Lay a tortilla on a parchment square. Put about 2 tablespoons lamb down the center, and top with 1 teaspoon guacamole and a cilantro sprig. Using the parchment, fold the tortilla in half and transfer to a serving plate. Repeat until all the ingredients are used, then arrange the tacos side by side so that they hold one another up. Serve the remaining guacamole and the braising liquid on the side.

THESE MEATBALLS ARE A LA PALAPA FIESTA FAVORITE, mostly because they taste so good, but also because they can be made in advance and reheated. The adobo is a thick, chile-based sauce that is used to baste and braise the meatballs and as a table sauce. This adobo recipe also makes a good salsa for serving alongside tacos, quesadillas, and many other dishes. The *albóndigas* can be made with beef only or pork only, or you can use ¾ pound beef and ¼ pound chorizo (page 141).

meatballs in chipotle chile with avocado-tomatillo salsa

ALBÓNDIGAS AL CHIPOTLE CON GUACASALSA

SERVES 6

MEATBALLS

½ pound ground beef

½ pound ground pork

1 tablespoon chopped fresh Mexican oregano leaves, or 1 teaspoon dried Mexican oregano

1 tablespoon chopped fresh mint leaves

1 teaspoon kosher salt

½ teaspoon freshly ground black pepper

ADOBO

6 pasilla chiles, seeded and membranes removed

6 guajillo chiles, seeded and membranes removed

2 cups hot water, or more as needed

4 plum tomatoes, coarsely chopped

3 chipotles en adobo with most of the adobo wiped off

6 cloves garlic

1 tablespoon chopped fresh oregano leaves, or 1 teaspoon dried oregano

1½ teaspoons freshly ground black pepper

1½ teaspoons ground cumin

1½ teaspoons ground cloves

½ cup corn oil

1 cup water

2 bay leaves

1 teaspoon chopped fresh thyme leaves, or ½ teaspoon dried thyme

2 teaspoons kosher salt

½ cup Avocado-Tomatillo Salsa (page 28)

½ cup chopped fresh cilantro leaves

To make the meatballs, in a large bowl, mix together the beef, pork, oregano, mint, salt, and pepper. Between dampened palms, roll meatballs about 1½ inches in diameter. Do not handle the mixture too much or the meatballs will be tough. Put the meatballs on a plate, cover, and refrigerate.

To make the adobo, in a bowl, combine the *pasilla* and *guajillo* chiles, add the 2 cups hot water, or more as needed to cover, and let stand for about 20 minutes to soften. Drain, reserving 2 cups of the water, and transfer the chiles to a food processor. Add the reserved water and process until the mixture is the consistency of tomato paste. You may have to do this in batches. Transfer to a nonreactive bowl.

Put the tomatoes, chipotle chiles, garlic, oregano, pepper, cumin, and cloves in the food processor (no need to rinse it) and process until smooth. Add to the chile paste and mix well.

In a stockpot, heat the oil over medium heat until a drop of the adobo sizzles on contact. Add the chile-tomato mixture and fry, stirring constantly, for about 4 minutes, or until the mixture turns a deep red, indicating the tomatoes are cooked.

Strain the sauce through a coarse-mesh sieve and return to the pot. Add the water and bring to a boil over medium-high heat. Add the bay leaves, thyme, and salt, stir well, and adjust the heat to maintain a simmer. Drop the chilled meatballs into the adobo and simmer for about 15 minutes, or until cooked through.

To serve, using a slotted spoon, transfer the meatballs to a serving platter. Spoon the adobo remaining in the pot into a small bowl and the salsa into a second small bowl. Sprinkle the meatballs with the cilantro and serve with the salsa and adobo.

WE GOT HOOKED ON *CHALUPAS* when we ate them laden with a variety of spicy fillings on the sun-splashed balcony of the spectacular Sotavento Hotel, in Zihuatanejo. The hotel, which is perched above the white sand Playa la Ropa and commands breathtaking views of the Pacific Ocean, was the perfect place to indulge in these popular *antojitos*. Back home at La Palapa, we memorialized that sunny setting by filling *chalupas* with our spicy house-made chorizo. This an easy and delicious recipe to double.

corn masa boats with chorizo
CHALUPAS CON CHORIZO

MAKES 12 CHALUPAS; SERVES 6

- 1 teaspoon corn oil
- ¾ cup Guajillo-Spiked Pork Chorizo (page 141)
- 12 Chalupas (page 140)
- ¼ cup La Palapa's Tomatillo Salsa (page 25)
- ¼ cup Crema Mexicana (page 139)
- 1 tablespoon finely crumbled queso fresco or ricotta salata cheese
- 1 tablespoon finely chopped onion
- 1 tablespoon finely chopped fresh cilantro leaves
- ½ cup La Palapa's Classic Guacamole (page 14)

In a skillet, heat the oil over medium heat. Add the chorizo and cook, breaking it into small pieces as you do, for about 5 minutes, or until cooked through. Transfer to a plate.

Warm the *chalupas* as directed and arrange on a platter. Fill each *chalupa* with about 1 tablespoon chorizo and top with 1 teaspoon salsa, 1 teaspoon *crema*, and about ¼ teaspoon each cheese, onion, and cilantro. Serve right away, with the guacamole on the side.

Cumpleaños | BIRTHDAY

We love to celebrate birthdays at La Palapa, and we give them the special attention they deserve. If someone makes a reservation for a large group, we always ask if they are celebrating anything. Most often it's a birthday. We fuss over the party and send something special to each guest, and everyone ends up having a good time.

This festive *taquiza* (taco feast) is perfect for a birthday celebration. But if there is no birthday on your calendar, it is also a good menu for a great cocktail party anytime. In addition to the cocktails and food, have plenty of ice-cold Mexican beer on hand.

SERVES 12 TO 18

margarita de flor de jamaica
HIBISCUS MARGARITA (PAGE 4)

paloma de mango y mezcal
MANGO-MEZCAL PALOMA (PAGE 6)

cacahuates enchilados
SPICY ROASTED PEANUTS (PAGE 18)

aceitunas sazonadas
SEASONED OLIVES (PAGE 18)

guacamole con tomatillo y durazno
GUACAMOLE WITH TOMATILLO AND PEACH (PAGE 15)

totopos de la palapa
LA PALAPA'S TORTILLA CHIPS (PAGE 15)

salsa tapatía de molcajete
MORTAR-CRUSHED TOMATO SALSA (PAGE 27)

salsa de chile serrano torreado
CHARRED SERRANO CHILE SALSA (PAGE 22)

salsa xnipec
PICKLED RED ONION AND HABANERO CHILE SALSA (PAGE 36)

tacos de pollo rostizado al achiote
ROAST ACHIOTE-RUBBED CHICKEN TACOS (PAGE 62)

tacos de pescado de la palapa
LA PALAPA'S FISH TACOS (PAGE 47)

tacos de puerco rostizado
ROAST PORK TACOS (PAGE 94)

THIS IS ONE OF OUR TOP RECOMMENDATIONS for a dinner party. Most of the components of this taco feast can be made in advance, leaving you with only the finishing touches before serving. In fact, the adobo, which is also excellent with chicken, duck, or beef, tastes best if made ahead and allowed to mellow for a day. We like to wrap the tacos in parchment paper for easy serving, but you can omit this step.

roast pork tacos
TACOS DE PUERCO ROSTIZADO

MAKES 12 TACOS; SERVES 6

ADOBO

2 ancho chiles, seeded and membranes removed

6 pasilla chiles, seeded and membranes removed

2 árbol chiles

½ cup olive oil

¼ cup honey

2 tablespoons sherry vinegar

1 teaspoon kosher salt

½ teaspoon freshly ground black pepper

1 fresh or dried avocado leaf or bay leaf

PORK

2 pork tenderloins, 1 to 1½ pounds each

¼ cup olive oil

2 cloves garlic, minced

½ teaspoon freshly ground black pepper

3 fresh or dried avocado leaves or bay leaves

1 teaspoon kosher salt

1 cup La Palapa's Tomatillo Salsa (page 25)

12 (6-inch) corn tortillas

12 romaine lettuce leaves

1 avocado, halved, pitted, peeled, and cut lengthwise into 12 slices

Pinch of kosher salt

To make the adobo, in a bowl, combine the chiles with hot water to cover and set aside for 20 minutes to soften. Drain and reserve ½ cup of the soaking water.

Transfer the chiles and the ½ cup water to a blender or food processor and process until smooth. Add the oil, honey, vinegar, salt, and pepper and pulse until well blended. Transfer to a nonreactive bowl, add the avocado leaf, and stir gently. Use immediately, or cover and refrigerate for up to 2 weeks.

To cook the pork, place the tenderloins in a shallow dish, and rub evenly with the oil, garlic, and pepper. Lay the avocado leaves on top, cover, and refrigerate for at least 8 hours or up to 12 hours. Remove from the refrigerator, rub the salt evenly over the pork, and let rest at room temperature for about 20 minutes before roasting. Meanwhile, preheat the oven to 400°F.

Lay the tenderloins in a deep, nonstick roasting pan, place in the oven, and cook for about 5 minutes on each side to sear. Baste the pork on all sides with some of the adobo, roast for about 10 minutes longer, and then baste again with more adobo. Cover with aluminum foil and roast for 8 to 10 minutes longer, or until an instant-read thermometer inserted into the thickest part of a tenderloin registers 155°F, or the meat juices run clear when a tenderloin is pierced.

Transfer to a cutting board and let rest for 10 minutes, then cut into 1-inch cubes. (You will only need about 1½ cups cubed pork; slice the remainder and use for sandwiches.)

While the pork is resting, process the tomatillo salsa in the blender until smooth and pour into a bowl. Warm the tortillas (see page 130).

Cut twelve 6-inch squares of parchment paper. Lay a tortilla on a parchment square. Put about 2 tablespoons pork down the center, and top with a spoonful of salsa, a lettuce leaf, an avocado slice, and a tiny pinch of salt. Using the parchment, fold in half and transfer to a serving plate. Repeat until all the ingredients are used, then arrange the tacos side by side on the plate so they hold one another up. Serve right away.

EVEN THOUGH YOU COOK THESE RIBS IN THE OVEN and not on the grill, they are great outdoor summertime food—messy and sticky, just as good ribs should be. They are best eaten with a cold *mojito*, a stack of warm tortillas, and platters of Sweet Plantains with Crema (page 121), Market-Style Corn on the Cob (page 114), and Grilled Spring Onions with Sea Salt and Lime (page 126).

pork ribs in a mulato chile adobo

COSTILLITAS AL ADOBO DE CHILE MULATO

SERVES 6

ADOBO

12 mulato chiles, seeded and membranes removed

1 poblano chile, seeded and membranes removed

½ onion, chopped

2 plum tomatoes

¼ cup corn oil

1 cup grated piloncillo or firmly packed light brown sugar

½ cup olive oil

¼ cup sherry vinegar

1 tablespoon kosher salt

1 teaspoon freshly ground black pepper

2 fresh or dried avocado leaves or bay leaves

3 pounds baby back pork ribs

2 cups pulque (see page 105) or Mexican beer, such as Tecate or Negra Modelo

6 black peppercorns

2 bay leaves

2 sprigs epazote or flat-leaf parsley

2 tablespoons kosher salt

1 teaspoon dried thyme, or 1 tablespoon chopped fresh thyme leaves

½ cup chopped fresh cilantro leaves

To make the adobo, in a small bowl, combine the *mulato* chiles with hot water to cover and let stand for about 20 minutes to soften. Drain and reserve ½ cup of the soaking water.

Transfer the *mulato* chiles to a blender, add the poblano chile and the ½ cup reserved water, and process until smooth. Add the onion and tomatoes and process until smooth and pastelike.

In a sauté pan, heat the corn oil over medium heat. Add the chile paste and cook, stirring constantly, for about 5 minutes, or until it is uniformly dark. Add the *piloncillo*, olive oil, vinegar, salt, and pepper, stir well, and heat, stirring constantly, for about 1 minute, or until uniformly hot. Remove from the heat, transfer to a nonreactive bowl, add the avocado leaves, stir gently, and let cool. (You will not need all of the adobo. Store the remainder in a tightly lidded container in the refrigerator for up to 2 weeks, and use for slathering over meats for grilling or as a salsa.)

To prepare the ribs, cut the racks into groups of 3 to 5 ribs, to make it easier to fit them into a pot. In a large stockpot, combine the ribs, pulque, peppercorns, bay leaves, epazote, salt, thyme, and water to cover. Bring to a boil over high heat, lower the heat to a steady simmer, and cook, uncovered, for about 45 minutes, or until the meat is partially cooked and the juices run

CONTINUED ▶

clear when the meat is pierced with a knife tip. Remove the ribs from the pot and pat dry with paper towels. Discard the cooking liquid.

Preheat the oven to 350°F. Heat a large, nonstick skillet over medium-high heat. Working in batches to avoid crowding, add the ribs and cook for about 3 minutes on each side, or until browned.

Transfer to a roasting pan and brush on both sides with some of the adobo. Roast, basting every 10 minutes with the pan juices, for about 1 hour, or until cooked through and tender.

Transfer to a platter, garnish with the cilantro, and serve right away.

PULQUE

This alcoholic drink, made from the sap of the maguey cactus, has been drunk since long before the Spaniards arrived in Mexico. Indeed, back then only high priests and community elders were allowed to consume pulque, and it played an important role in religious ceremonies and festivals, especially those associated with fertility. At first, the Spaniards prohibited pulque because of its importance to pre-Catholic rituals. Eventually they relented, but they continued to control its consumption by setting up *pulquerias* where its purchase was subject to tariffs.

Despite such efforts to discourage its use, pulque continues to have an important role in Mexican culture, with many rituals associated with both its fermentation and its consumption. For example, some workers in pulque factories still recite the Lord's Prayer as they pour the fermented sap, called *aguamiel*, or "honey water," into a batch of pulque. The practice has nothing to do with religion, however. Instead, the workers measure the amount of sap necessary for fermentation by pouring just as long as it takes to recite the prayer. Also, many workers believe that women should not be allowed near the fermentation area because their presence will adversely alter the quality of the pulque.

Pulquerias, typically found in old neighborhoods, remain the traditional place to drink pulque. Patrons often consume it as a way to remember ancestors and loved ones. According to an old saying, "*Entrar a una pulqueria es conocer historias de amor y abandono y escuchar a musicos cantando sin parar*" (To enter a *pulqueria* is to hear musicians sing stories of great love and great heartbreak).

Pulque is a popular libation at weddings and other celebrations as well, where it is usually drunk out of *jicaras* (dried gourds). It may also be *curado* (flavored), or added to fruit juice to make *tepaches* (fermented fruit drinks). It is used in the kitchen, too, primarily in marinades, braising liquids, or salsas, where it is said to make the dish *borracha*, or "drunken."

To make about 4 cups of *tepache de piña*, or fermented pineapple juice, peel and core 1 ripe pineapple. Cut the flesh into chunks, transfer to a food processor, and process until liquefied. Measure 2 cups of the pineapple juice and pour into a glass jar or other nonreactive container. Add 2 cups of pulque, stir well, and refrigerate for 8 to 12 hours to give the juice time to ferment. Serve chilled.

MEXICAN-STYLE FONDUES, or *fundidos*, are popular throughout the country, and they charm our guests, as well. If you haven't tried this oven-baked dish of melted cheese and chorizo, served with a basket of warm tortillas, don't wait another day. The tortillas are used to scoop up the molten mixture, and a bowl of fresh salsa is the perfect accompaniment. You can bake the fundido in any ovenproof dish or in individual ramekins. Don't forget to warm the tortillas while the *fundido* cooks.

cheese baked with guajillo-spiked chorizo
QUESO FUNDIDO CON CHORIZO

SERVES 6

- 1 teaspoon corn oil
- ½ pound Guajillo-Spiked Pork Chorizo (page 141), store-bought chorizo, or other spicy sausage, casings removed
- 3 cups finely shredded Monterey Jack cheese
- 1 cup grated queso Cotija, queso añejo, or queso manchego
- 12 (6-inch) flour or corn tortillas
- La Palapa's Tomatillo Salsa (page 25)

Preheat the oven to 375°F. In a large skillet, heat the oil over medium heat. Add the chorizo and cook, breaking it into small pieces as you do, for about 5 minutes, or until cooked through. Transfer to a plate.

In a bowl, mix together the cheeses.

Oil an 8-inch square flameproof baking dish with 1-inch sides; a 6-cup flameproof baking or gratin dish no more than 1½ inches deep; or 6 (8-ounce) flameproof ramekins. If using ramekins, place on a rimmed baking sheet.

Spread about half of the cheese in the baking dish or evenly among the ramekins. Bake for about 6 minutes for the single dish or 2 minutes for the ramekins, or until the cheese starts to melt. Remove from the oven and scatter the chorizo over the cheese. Top with the rest of the cheese and bake for about 5 minutes longer, or until the cheese melts.

Remove from the oven and turn on the broiler. Slide the baking dish or ramekins under the broiler for about 2 minutes, or until the cheese is lightly browned.

Meanwhile, warm the tortillas (see page 130), transfer them to a basket, and cover with a kitchen towel or cloth napkin to keep warm.

Serve the bubbling-hot *fundido* with the salsa and the tortillas.

MARGARITTE CAME UP WITH THIS miniature corn bread sandwich when we were planning the menu for an elegant cocktail party. We call it a *torta*, although it's not a traditional one because it calls for tiny corn bread muffins, rather than large *telera* bread. The flavors of the ham, cheese, and avocado melt together in the mouth, and the corn bread imparts an addictive aftertaste. The corn bread muffins are also excellent on their own, served with chipotle honey (see Cook's Note).

serrano ham, cheese, and avocado sandwich on poblano corn bread

TORTAS DE JAMÓN SERRANO Y QUESO CHIHUAHUA EN PANECILLO DE ELOTE

MAKES 24 SANDWICHES; SERVES 6 TO 8

CORN BREAD

Vegetable oil spray (optional)

⅓ cup plus 1 tablespoon corn oil

2 poblano chiles, seeded, membranes removed, and finely chopped

2 cups yellow cornmeal

1½ teaspoons kosher salt

½ teaspoon baking powder

¾ cup whole milk

1 (8-ounce) can corn kernels, or 1¼ cups thawed, frozen corn kernels

2 large eggs

1 tablespoon sugar

TORTAS

½ cup Chipotle Crema (page 36)

½ pound jamón serrano or prosciutto, thinly sliced

½ pound queso Chihuahua or Muenster cheese, thinly sliced

1 avocado, halved, pitted, peeled, and thinly sliced

24 large, nice-looking fresh cilantro leaves

To make the corn bread, preheat the oven to 450°F. Coat 24 mini muffin cups with vegetable oil spray, or line with paper liners.

In a sauté pan, heat the 1 tablespoon oil over medium heat until a piece of chile dropped into the pan sizzles on contact. Add the chiles and cook for about 5 minutes, or until softened. Transfer to a bowl and set aside to cool.

In a large bowl, whisk together the cornmeal, salt, and baking powder.

In a blender, combine the milk, corn kernels, eggs, sugar, and the remaining ⅓ cup oil and process until the corn is pureed and the mixture is nearly smooth.

Add the corn mixture to the dry ingredients and mix just until evenly moistened. Fold in the cooled chiles. Spoon the batter into the prepared muffin cups, filling each cup about half full.

Bake for 20 to 25 minutes, or until a toothpick inserted into the center of a muffin comes out clean. Let the muffins cool in the pans on wire racks, then remove them from the pans. If you have used paper liners, peel them off the muffins.

To make the *tortas*, using a serrated knife, cut each corn muffin in half crosswise. Put a small dollop of the *crema* on the bottom half of the muffin, layer with a slice each of ham, cheese, and avocado, and top with a cilantro leaf. Cover with the top half of the muffin, and spear with a decorative toothpick to hold the *torta* together. Repeat to make 24 sandwiches. Serve right away.

COOK'S NOTE: *For a delicious treat, in a small bowl, whisk together ½ cup honey and 2 teaspoons adobo from a can of chipotles en adobo. Set aside for at least 15 minutes to allow the flavors to blend. Or, if not using right away, cover and refrigerate for up to 2 weeks. Split the corn bread muffins and spread with the honey.*

MARGARITTE MADE THIS CHILLED SOUP for a family get-together, and it was such a hit, we decided to serve it at La Palapa, where we added the spiced green pumpkin seeds for crunch. It has become one of our most requested party dishes and a favorite menu item. Because drinking just a few sips hits the spot on a hot day, we often serve it in shot glasses with a light sprinkling of the pumpkin seeds. Or, sometimes we use cocktail glasses, espresso cups, or even small ramekins.

chilled avocado soup

SOPA DE AGUACATE Y PEPITAS

SERVES 6

3 large avocados, halved, pitted, peeled, and coarsely chopped

3 cups low-sodium chicken broth

1 to 2 cups heavy cream

2 tablespoons freshly squeezed lime juice

Coarse salt and freshly ground black pepper

1 teaspoon canola oil

½ cup green pumpkin seeds (pepitas)

1½ teaspoons kosher salt

Chipotle chile powder

In a blender, combine the avocadoes, broth, and 1 cup cream and process until smooth and the consistency of a thick cream soup. (You may have to work in batches.) Add more cream (up to 1 cup) as needed to achieve the correct consistency.

Transfer to a bowl and season with the lime juice, coarse salt, and pepper. Cover and refrigerate for about 1 hour, or until chilled.

In a nonstick or cast-iron skillet, heat the oil over medium heat. Add the pumpkin seeds and toss for about 20 seconds, or until they darken a shade and are fragrant. Add the kosher salt and a little chile powder (it is spicy, so start with just a tiny pinch) and toss to coat the seeds evenly. Pour onto a plate and let cool.

Taste the soup and adjust the seasoning. Ladle into bowls (or into smaller vessels as described in the head-note for twice as many servings) and sprinkle with the pumpkin seeds and a little bit more chile powder, if you like. Serve at once.

EVERY FALL, we eagerly await the arrival of large burlap bags filled with glorious Mexican squashes, or *calabazas*. They vary in color from gold to green to orange, and each is slightly different in size and shape. When we watch the squashes tumble out of the bags, we feel as if the Mexican harvest has arrived at our Manhattan doorstep. If you do not have access to traditional Mexican squashes, butternut or kabocha squash is a good substitute.

Both *calabazas* and this velvety soup made from them are central to the celebration of Día de los Muertos. During the festival, the squash is candied with raw sugar (*piloncillo*) and served with *crema* and *queso fresco* for a perfect balance of sweet and savory.

squash soup with crema and toasted almonds

SOPA DE CALABAZA CON CREMA Y ALMENDRAS

SERVES 6

½ cup slivered blanched almonds

2 pounds calabaza or other winter squash, such as butternut or kabocha

½ cup (1 stick) unsalted butter

½ onion, sliced

½ jalapeño chile, seeded and membranes removed

6 cups water

1 whole clove

1 (3-inch) stick Mexican cinnamon

1 teaspoon cornstarch

1 tablespoon lukewarm water

2 cups heavy cream

6 tablespoons firmly packed light or dark brown sugar

Kosher salt

In a heavy, dry skillet, toast the almonds over medium heat, stirring constantly with a wooden spoon, for about 3 minutes, or until aromatic and golden brown. Pour onto a plate and let cool.

Using a vegetable peeler or small paring knife, peel the squash, cut in half, and scoop out the seeds. Cut the flesh into 2- to 3-inch pieces.

In a stockpot, melt the butter over medium-high heat. Add the onion and chile and sauté for about 5 minutes, or until the onion is golden but not browned. Add the squash and sauté for 6 to 7 minutes longer, or until the squash begins to soften.

Add the water, clove, and cinnamon and bring to a boil. Reduce the heat and simmer, uncovered, for 10 minutes, or until the squash is very soft. Adjust the heat as needed to maintain a steady simmer.

Remove from the heat, discard the clove and cinnamon, and let cool for about 15 minutes. Then, working in batches, transfer the soup to a blender or food processor and process until smooth. Do not fill the blender too full, as the hot liquid can expand and overflow.

Return the blended ingredients to the stockpot. In a small bowl or cup, dissolve the cornstarch in the luke-warm water to make a slurry. Add the slurry, cream, and brown sugar to the pot, whisk well, and then reheat the soup slowly over low heat, whisking con-stantly. Season with salt. (At this point, the soup can be cooled, transfered to a lidded container, and stored in the refrigerator for up to 1 week. Reheat just before serving.)

Ladle into bowls (or into smaller vessels such as espresso cups, small ramekins, or shot glasses for twice as many servings) and garnish with the toasted almonds. Serve right away.

COOK'S NOTE: *If you enclose the cinnamon and clove in a small cheesecloth sack, tied with butcher's twine, they will be easy to remove from the soup.*

MARGARITTE WAS INSPIRED to create this elegant, festive salad—a good accompaniment for nearly any meal—by the fresh fruit carts seen in the plazas of most Mexican towns. You can also opt to omit the lettuce and cilantro and serve the fruits and jicama as crudités. Either way, this recipe is quick and easy to make and, of course, delicious. If you want to tame the heat but keep the color, use paprika in place of the chile powder.

jicama, melon, and pineapple salad

ENSALADILLA DE JÍCAMA Y FRUTAS

SERVES 6

1 jicama, peeled and cut into batons 2 to 3 inches long and about ½ inch thick (about 1 cup)

½ cup freshly squeezed orange juice

Kosher salt

2 oranges

1 Granny Smith apple, cored and cut into wedges about ½ inch thick (about 1 cup)

¼ cantaloupe, peeled, seeded, and cut into wedges about ½ inch thick (about 1 cup)

½ small pineapple, peeled, cored, and cut into wedges about ½ inch thick (about 1 cup)

3 tablespoons chopped fresh cilantro leaves

2 romaine lettuce hearts, leaves separated

2 tablespoons freshly squeezed lime juice

⅛ to 1 teaspoon piquín chile powder or sweet Spanish paprika

In a small bowl, combine the jicama, orange juice, and ¼ teaspoon salt and toss to mix. Cover and refrigerate for 1 hour. Do not marinate any longer; the salt will make the jicama limp.

Cut a slice off the top and bottom of 1 orange to expose the flesh. Stand the orange upright on a cutting board. Using a sharp knife, and following the contour of the fruit, slice off the peel, pith, and membrane in wide strips. Holding the fruit over a bowl, cut along both sides of each section to free it from the membrane, letting the sections drop into the bowl. Repeat with the remaining orange.

In a bowl, combine the jicama and its juices, the orange sections, the apple, cantaloupe, pineapple, and cilantro and toss to mix.

Line a large serving bowl with the romaine leaves. Mound the fruit mixture in the center of the lined bowl and sprinkle with the lime juice and with the chile powder and salt to taste. Use a light hand; the chile powder is spicy. Serve immediately.

THIS SALAD HAS BEEN ON OUR MENU since the day we opened the doors. It makes a great meal served with grilled shrimp or chicken or with poached chicken breasts. You can top it with croutons (page 112) for a little crunch to offset the creaminess of the avocado.

Barbara first tasted this dish as a child. She was a frequent guest at the home of her friends Gonzalo and Rodrigo, where this salad, prepared by their mother, Mercedes García Barcha, wife of famed author Gabriel García Marquez, was often on the menu. Mercedes is an inspiring cook who shares our love of avocado and hearts of palm.

hearts of palm salad with fresh oregano vinaigrette
ENSALADA DE PALMITOS

SERVES 6

VINAIGRETTE
¼ cup loosely packed fresh Mexican oregano leaves
1 shallot, chopped
1 teaspoon kosher salt
½ teaspoon freshly ground black pepper
⅓ cup sherry vinegar
1 tablespoon sherry
1 cup extra virgin olive oil

SALAD
1 head Boston lettuce
½ cup (¾-inch-thick) slices hearts of palm
½ cup chopped plum tomato
½ cup chopped avocado

To make the dressing, in a blender, combine the oregano, shallot, salt, and pepper and process until smooth. With the motor running, slowly add the vinegar and sherry. Then add the oil in a slow, steady stream and process until the vinaigrette emulsifies. Taste and adjust the seasoning with salt, if needed. Use immediately, or cover and refrigerate for up to 1 week. Shake or stir well before using. You will need only ½ cup of the vinaigrette for this salad. Reserve the remainder for another use.

To make the salad, tear the lettuce into pieces about 2 inches. (If you tear the leaves, you are less likely to bruise them than if you cut them with a knife.) Transfer to a salad bowl and add the hearts of palm and tomato.

Drizzle the salad with about ½ cup of the vinaigrette and toss to coat evenly. Scatter the avocado over the top and serve.

PURSLANE IS TYPICAL of the many wild greens found in Mexican kitchens. It works beautifully in this salad, where the sweetness of the pineapple offsets the tartness of the purslane, and the creaminess of the *queso fresco* brings both elements together in harmony. We usually season this salad with coarse salt from the town of Zihuatanejo, but kosher salt works well, too.

purslane salad with pineapple and pecans
ENSALADA DE VERDOLAGAS CON PIÑA Y NUEZ

SERVES 6

1 cup pecan halves or coarsely chopped pecans

4 cups loosely packed purslane leaves

½ small pineapple, peeled, cored, and cubed (about 1 cup)

Juice of 2 limes

Kosher salt or sea salt

¾ cup crumbled queso fresco, feta cheese, or ricotta salata cheese

In a heavy, dry skillet, toast the pecans over medium heat, stirring constantly, for about 1 minute, or until aromatic and lightly browned. Pour onto a plate and let cool.

In a salad bowl, toss together the purslane and pineapple. Add the lime juice, toss to mix, and season to taste with salt. Garnish with the cheese and toasted pecans and serve right away.

SEVERAL COMPETING STORIES chronicle the origin of this iconic salad, but the most popular one credits César Cardini with creating it in the kitchen of his Caesar's restaurant in Tijuana, in the early 1920s. His salad included romaine lettuce, garlic, cheese, Worcestershire sauce, and coddled eggs, but no anchovies. We don't use eggs or Worcestershire sauce, but the anchovies are critical in the salad and in the dressing—an idea we owe to our friend Ellen Smith, who one day made a salad similar to this one that caught our fancy.

traditional césar salad

ENSALADA CÉSAR

SERVES 6

CROUTONS

2 cups cubed crusty bread, such as bolillo or baguette

2 tablespoons sweet Spanish paprika

1 tablespoon kosher salt

½ teaspoon piquín chile powder or cayenne pepper

½ cup olive oil

DRESSING

1½ cups extra virgin olive oil

¼ cup white wine vinegar

¼ cup freshly squeezed lime juice (about 2 limes)

3 cloves garlic

3 anchovy fillets, chopped

½ cup pine nuts

3 romaine hearts, outer leaves removed

½ cup thinly shaved queso Cotija or Parmesan cheese

6 anchovy fillets

To make the croutons, preheat the oven to 350°F. In a large bowl, toss the bread with the paprika, salt, and chile powder. Drizzle the bread cubes with the oil while shaking the bowl. (Stirring can squash the cubes.)

Spread the cubes evenly on a rimmed baking sheet and bake for about 5 minutes, or until they begin to brown. Remove the baking sheet from the oven, turn the cubes over, and bake for about 4 minutes longer, or until crispy and nicely browned. Check several times during baking to prevent scorching. Slide the croutons onto a plate and let cool. (You need only 1 cup croutons for this salad; reserve the remainder for another use. They will keep in a tightly covered container at room temperature for up to 1 week.)

To make the dressing, in a blender or food processor, combine the oil, vinegar, lime juice, garlic, and anchovies and process for about 5 minutes, or until emulsified and creamy. (You need only 1 cup dressing for this salad; reserve the remainder for another use. It will keep in the refrigerator for up to 1 week.)

In a heavy, dry skillet, toast the pine nuts over medium heat, stirring constantly, for 30 seconds to 1 minute, or until aromatic and lightly browned. Pour onto a plate and let cool. If not using right away, store in a tightly covered jar in the refrigerator for up to 2 weeks.

In a large salad bowl, toss together the romaine leaves, pine nuts, and 1 cup of the croutons. Drizzle with 1 cup of the dressing and toss well. Top with the cheese and anchovy fillets and serve right away.

THIS RECIPE, like the one for *chalupas* with chorizo (page 90), was inspired by a visit to the seaside town of Zihuatanejo, where *chalupas* are a local specialty. When we returned to New York, Margaritte added this recipe to the menu. It has been a great favorite with our customers ever since. *Chalupas* have a nice crispness that makes a good counterpoint to the soft, salty beans, the smooth *crema*, and the bright tomatillo salsa.

corn masa boats stuffed with pinto beans and tomatillo salsa

CHALUPAS CON FRIJOLES PINTOS Y SALSA VERDE

MAKES 12 CHALUPAS; SERVES 6

¾ cup Slow-Cooked Vegetarian Pinto Beans (page 146)

3 tablespoons corn oil

¼ cup La Palapa's Tomatillo Salsa (page 25)

¼ cup Crema Mexicana (page 139)

1 tablespoon crumbled queso fresco or finely shredded Monterey Jack cheese

1 tablespoon chopped onion

1 tablespoon chopped fresh cilantro leaves

12 Chalupas (page 140)

Set a skillet over medium-high heat, add the beans and oil, and heat, stirring occasionally, for about 10 minutes, or until heated through. Transfer to a small bowl.

Meanwhile, put the salsa, *crema*, cheese, onion, and cilantro in separate small bowls.

Warm the *chalupas* as directed and arrange on a platter. Fill each *chalupa* with 1 tablespoon pinto beans and top with 1 teaspoon salsa, a dollop of *crema*, and a sprinkling each of the cheese, onion, and cilantro. Serve right away.

THERE IS A LOVELY AREA IN MEXICO CITY called Xochimilco, where the canals and gardens of the ancient Aztec city of Tenochtitlán still exist. Families gather in these floating gardens on weekends to picnic and enjoy the surrounding beauty. Corn sellers paddle along the canals, offering this corn straight from the small charcoal grills in their canoes. Other boats offer nosegays of fragrant gardenias, and still others sell tostadas and *doraditas*. Marimba players and mariachi bands add to the festive spirit. When we cannot make it to the gardens, we buy *elote del mercado* from Mexico City's San Angel market, where we routinely go to buy chiles and baskets.

market-style corn on the cob
ELOTE DEL MERCADO

SERVES 6 TO 12

- ½ cup grated queso Cotija or Parmesan cheese
- 1 teaspoon piquín chile powder
- 12 ears of corn in their husks
- 12 cups (3 quarts) water
- 2 tablespoons sugar
- 2 tablespoons kosher salt
- Vegetable oil spray
- 2 limes, halved
- ½ cup mayonnaise

In a shallow bowl, mix together the cheese and chile powder. Set aside.

Remove the outer leaves and silk from each ear of corn, leaving a single layer of leaves to protect the kernels.

In an 8-quart stockpot, bring the water to a boil over high heat. Add the sugar and salt and stir to dissolve, then add the corn. When the water returns to a boil, let the corn cook for about 5 minutes, or until tender.

Meanwhile, prepare a medium-hot fire in a charcoal or gas grill. Before igniting the grill, lightly coat the grill grid with vegetable oil spray to prevent sticking.

Using tongs, lift the ears of corn from the water, pausing to let the excess water drain back into the pot. Wrap each ear in a sheet of aluminum foil. Place the foil packets on the grill grid, and grill for about 10 minutes, turning every 3 minutes, until the kernels are lightly browned. To check for doneness, partially unwrap 1 ear and check the color. Remove the ears from the grill, and then remove the foil.

Pull the leaves down to create a handle for the corn. Rub the lime halves over the kernels, then spread the mayonnaise evenly over the kernels. Coat the ears with the cheese mixture and serve right away.

THESE GORGEOUS CRÊPES filled with seasoned *huitlacoche* represent a perfect marriage of European cooking techniques with indigenous ingredients. (For more on *huitlacoche*, see page 117.) You can assemble these crêpes a day ahead, refrigerate them, and then pop them into the oven just before serving. You will have more *huitlacoche* filling than you need for the crêpes. The remainder can be added to omelets, quesadillas, or *chalupas* for easy *antojitos*.

huitlacoche crêpes

CREPAS DE HUITLACOCHE

MAKES 12 CRÊPES; SERVES 6 OR 12

HUITLACOCHE CORN MIXTURE
1 cup huitlacoche, fresh or canned
2 tablespoons corn oil
1 poblano chile
¼ cup chopped white onion
1 dried hoja santa leaf or fresh epazote leaf (optional)
1 cup fresh or thawed, frozen corn kernels

CREMA POBLANA
4 poblano chiles, seeded and membranes removed
1 jalapeño chile, seeded and membranes removed
1 cup chopped fresh cilantro leaves (about 1½ bunches)
¼ cup chopped white onion
1 clove garlic, chopped

3 tablespoons unsalted butter
2 tablespoons corn oil
1 cup grated queso Cotija, queso añejo, or Parmesan cheese
1 cup Crema Mexicana (page 139) or heavy cream
Kosher salt and freshly ground black pepper
12 crêpes (page 139)
1 cup shredded Monterey Jack cheese or queso Chihuahua

To make the *huitlacoche* corn mixture, put the *huitlacoche* in a blender or food processor and process just until chopped.

In a skillet, heat the oil over medium-high heat. Add the chile and onion and sauté for about 5 minutes, or until the onion is translucent. Stir in the *huitlacoche*, *hoja santa*, and corn kernels and remove from the heat. Set aside.

To make the *crema poblana*, in a food processor, combine the chiles, cilantro, onion, and garlic and process until pureed but with a little texture. Set aside.

In a sauté pan, melt the butter in the oil over medium heat. Add the *huitlacoche*-corn mixture and cook, stirring, for about 5 minutes, or until heated through. Bring to a simmer and cook for about 2 minutes longer.

Off the heat, fold in the *queso Cotija*. Return to medium-low heat and bring to a gentle simmer. Slowly whisk in the *crema* to thicken the mixture. Season with salt and pepper. (If you use *crema*, the sauce will be richer and saltier than if you use heavy cream.) Use right away, or let cool, cover tightly, and refrigerate for up to 5 days. Stir well before using.

To fill the crêpes, preheat the oven to 375°F. Have ready 6 flameproof individual gratin dishes or 12 smaller flameproof ramekins.

Lay 1 crêpe on a work surface, put about 2 tablespoons of the *huitlacoche* mixture in the center, and fold in the sides to create a parcel about 3 inches square. Repeat to make 12 parcels total. Put 2 parcels, seam side down, in each gratin dish, or 1 parcel in each ramekin. Top each parcel with about 2 tablespoons of the *crema poblana*, and then top evenly with the Jack cheese.

Transfer the dishes to a rimmed baking sheet and bake for about 15 minutes, or until hot. Turn off the oven and turn on the broiler. Slide the dishes under the broiler and broil for about 2 minutes, or until the cheese is lightly browned. Serve immediately.

HUITLACOCHE

In the United States, *huitlacoche* is known as corn smut, but in Mexico it is a delicacy, prized for its pungent, smoky-sweet flavor and served in the country's most sophisticated restaurants. The exotic mushroomy flavor of the fungus is sometimes compared to truffles and gloriously transforms a simple taco or quesadilla.

Until you taste *huitlacoche* (wheat-lah-KOH-chay), you may not believe how delicious this fungus is. It grows on all varieties of corn, and we always have it on the menu at La Palapa, where we serve it in many ways, including tucked into crêpes and quesadillas and in shrimp with tequila.

Most of the *huitlacoche* (sometimes spelled *cuitalacoche*) in the United States is imported from Mexico, usually canned or frozen, but a grower in Massachusetts is now cultivating it on organic corn, so we are able to get it fresh. The fungus grows in the kernels of sweet corn, which become large and oddly shaped and turn velvety gray or black as Nature marries mushroom and corn flavors.

ON MARKET DAY IN JUST ABOUT ANY MEXICAN TOWN, you will see merchants who sell corn kernels cut from the cobs, or *esquites*. A small cup of the hot, seasoned grain will fortify you as you walk through the aisles of bright, vibrant vegetables, fruits, herbs, and spices. This recipe combines the food traditions of central Mexico, where corn cultivation is the main staple, and the cheese-making traditions of northern Mexico, where dairy farms and wheatfields are commonplace. Because of the importance of wheat, we suggest serving flour tortillas with the *fundido*, though corn tortillas will be delicious, too.

cheese baked with corn and epazote
QUESO FUNDIDO DE ESQUITES

SERVES 6

Unsalted butter, for ramekins

1 (10-ounce) bag frozen white or yellow corn kernels

¼ cup corn oil

½ cup finely chopped onion

1 jalapeño chile, finely chopped

Kosher salt

¼ cup chopped epazote leaves or fresh flat-leaf parsley leaves

2 cups shredded Monterey Jack cheese or queso Chihuahua

1 cup grated queso Cotija or queso añejo

12 (6-inch) flour or corn tortillas

½ cup Mortar-Crushed Tomato Salsa (page 27)

1 cup Fresh Tomato Salsa (page 29)

Preheat the oven to 375°F. Butter 6 (8-ounce) flame-proof ramekins or custard cups and place on a rimmed baking sheet.

Cook the corn kernels according to the package directions, then drain well.

Meanwhile, in a stockpot, heat the oil over medium-high heat. Add the onion and chile and sauté for 3 to 5 minutes, or until the onion is translucent.

Add the drained corn to the onion and chile, stir well, and remove from the heat. Season with salt, and fold in the epazote.

In a bowl, mix together the cheeses. Divide about half of the cheese evenly among the ramekins.

Bake the ramekins for about 6 minutes, or until the cheese starts to melt. Remove from the oven, top with the corn mixture and the remaining cheese, and bake for about 5 minutes longer, or until the cheese melts and the corn is heated through. Meanwhile, warm the tortillas (see page 130), transfer them to a basket, and cover with a kitchen towel or cloth napkin to keep warm.

Remove the ramekins from the oven and turn on the broiler. Slide the ramekins under the broiler and broil for about 2 minutes, or until the cheese is lightly browned.

Remove from the broiler and serve the bubbling-hot *fundido* with the salsas and the tortillas.

IN OAXACA, a particularly delicious tamale pairs savory *mole negro* with sweet plantains. We use these same superb ingredients for a folded crêpe just sweet enough to intensify the flavors and serve it as a daily special, much to the delight of our customers.

crêpes with sweet plantains and oaxaca-style black mole

CREPAS CON MOLE NEGRO OAXAQUEÑO Y PLÁTANOS

MAKES 12 CRÊPES; SERVES 6

12 crêpes (page 139)

1½ cups cubed sweet plantains, without the crema (see page 121)

1½ cups Oaxaca-Style Black Mole (page 142)

1 cup shredded Monterey Jack cheese or queso Chihuahua

Preheat the oven to 375°F. Arrange 6 flameproof individual gratin dishes or 12 flameproof smaller ramekins on a rimmed baking sheet.

Lay 1 crêpe on a work surface, put about 2 tablespoons plantains in the center, and fold into a parcel about 3 inches square. Repeat until you have made 12 parcels total. Put 2 parcels in each gratin dish, or 1 parcel in each ramekin. Top each parcel with about 2 tablespoons mole, and then top evenly with cheese.

Transfer the dishes to a rimmed baking sheet and bake for about 15 minutes, or until hot. Turn off the oven and turn on the broiler. Slide the dishes under the broiler and broil for about 2 minutes, or until the cheese is lightly browned. Serve immediately.

GUESTS OFTEN ASK US how we cook plantains to make them so sublimely sweet, guessing that we add sugar. We don't. The key to the sweetness is cooking only fully ripened plantains: their skins must be completely black. At this point, all of their starch has been converted to sugar, and when correctly cooked, these natural sugars bloom and caramelize. The plantains are perfect foils for spicy foods. At La Palapa, we like to dip them in *crema* or a rich black mole. They can also be served as canapés or a side dish.

sweet plantains with crema
PLÁTANOS CON CREMA

SERVES 6

3 ripe plantains with black skin

Corn oil, for deep-frying

½ cup crumbled queso fresco or ricotta salata cheese

1 cup Crema Mexicana (page 139)

Peel the plantains and cut them on the diagonal into ½-inch-thick slices.

Pour the oil to a depth of 1 inch into a deep sauté pan and heat over medium-high heat to 350°F on a deep-frying thermometer, or until a plantain slice dropped into the oil sizzles on contact.

Working in batches to avoid crowding, fry the plantain slices for about 5 minutes, or until browned and caramelized on the outside and still soft on the inside. Using tongs or a slotted spoon, transfer to paper towels to drain. Let the oil regain temperature between batches.

Arrange the hot plantains on a platter and immediately sprinkle with the cheese so that it melts slightly. Serve the *crema* on the side for dipping.

Día de los Muertos / DAY OF THE DEAD

In Mexico, it is traditional to celebrate those who have died by eating and drinking the foods and beverages that most pleased them when they were alive. The ritual is not about grief and solemnity, but about drawing closer to one another through celebration and remembrance. The belief is that it also gives those who have gone a chance to see the people they left behind happy and at peace.

Día de los Muertos—Day of the Dead—stretches over the first two days of November, and it is celebrated in Mexico as nowhere else in the Catholic world. It is the most important festival of the year, especially in rural areas, where the preparations in anticipation of the event are a major preoccupation for months in advance.

At La Palapa, we take the Day of the Dead seriously and joyfully. We create the traditional sugar skulls fashioned all over Mexico and serve moles made with special chiles, such as *costeños, chilhuacles,* and *mulatos*. The Fiesta de Muertos has been called an intimate, melancholy celebration marked by a "strange gladness." It is also an exuberant, sensual, and remarkably life-affirming festival. We urge anyone who is in New York during the early November festival to join us.

Margaritas and our *sangrita* and tequila shots are perfect for a Day of the Dead party. After all, *sangrita* comes from the Spanish *sangre*, or "blood." The bright orange of the salmon ceviche provides a striking contrast to the black of the *huitlacoche* crêpes, and our devilish shrimp, which are sautéed in a chile-laced salsa, suit the spirit of the holiday perfectly. Browned, thick slices of sweet plantains with *crema* for dipping are a good balance for the spicy offerings.

SERVES 12

Life and Death are not contrary worlds. We are a single stem with two flowers.

—JUAN RULFO

BOTH CHOCOLATE AND VANILLA are indigenous to Mexico, and so it is no surprise our chocolate pudding is deep, dark, delicious, and a perfect ending to a traditional feast. This recipe was inspired by a pudding made by our longtime friend Eddie McGraw, who grew up in Texas and likes to eat at La Palapa because our food reminds him of the Mexican food he ate back home. For parties at La Palapa, we serve this pudding in small, delicate cordial glasses topped with whipped cream.

mexican chocolate pudding
CASUELITA DE CREMA DE CHOCOLATE

SERVES 12

1 cup granulated sugar

¼ cup unsweetened cocoa powder

¼ cup cornstarch

¼ cup all-purpose flour

Pinch of salt

6 cups whole milk

9 large egg yolks

½ cup heavy cream

1 tablespoon ancho chile powder or ancho chile paste (see page 133)

1 (3-inch) stick Mexican cinnamon (see Cook's Note)

3 ounces semisweet or bittersweet chocolate, coarsely chopped

WHIPPED CREAM

2 cups heavy cream

1 tablespoon confectioners' sugar

1 teaspoon pure vanilla extract, preferably Mexican

To make the pudding, in a large saucepan, whisk together the granulated sugar, cocoa powder, cornstarch, flour, and salt. Pour in 2 cups of the milk and, using a handheld mixer, beat on medium-high speed until smooth. Add the egg yolks and cream and beat until smooth. Then beat in the remaining 4 cups milk. Stir in the chile powder and cinnamon stick.

Set the saucepan over medium heat and whisk constantly until the mixture comes to a boil. Remove from the heat, add the chocolate to the hot mixture, and whisk until melted and the pudding mixture is evenly colored. Remove and discard the cinnamon.

Let the pudding cool. Pour into 12 (5-ounce) custard cups or ramekins. Alternatively, you can pour the pudding into a large bowl. Lay plastic wrap directly on the surface of the pudding to prevent a skin from forming, let cool, and refrigerate for at least 3 hours to chill, or for up to 5 days.

Just before serving, whip the cream. Fill the bottom of a large bowl with ice and nestle a smaller, metal bowl in it. (This ensures the cream will whip faster and easier.) Pour the cream into the smaller bowl and, using the handheld mixer, beat on medium-high speed until it begins to thicken. Add the confectioners' sugar and vanilla and continue beating until the cream forms nearly firm peaks.

Serve the pudding topped with generous dollops of whipped cream.

COOK'S NOTE: *Omit the cinnamon if you cannot find Mexican cinnamon, and omit the chile paste, if you like. The dessert will still be delicious.*

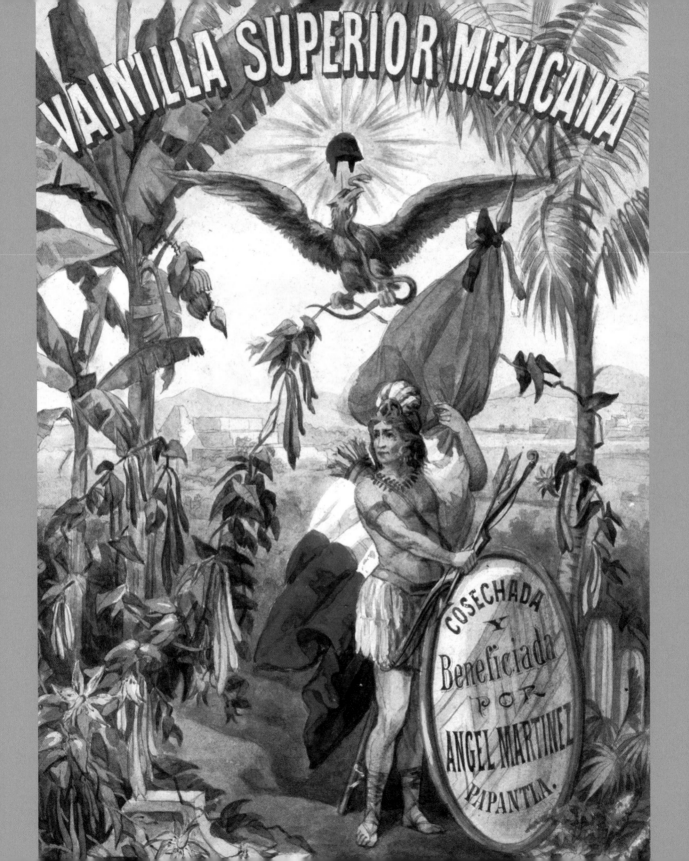

GRILLED SPRING ONIONS are sublime served with lime juice and sea salt. Eat them as is, or serve them alongside skirt steak or tucked into a grilled-steak taco. We use sweet spring onions from Mexico that have bulbs 1 to 2 inches across. If you find them in a Mexican market near you, try them. Otherwise, use the largest scallions you can find, so they won't dry out during grilling.

grilled spring onions with sea salt and lime

CEBOLLITAS ASADAS

SERVES 6

1½ pounds spring onions (about 6 bunches)
4 cups water
Kosher or coarse salt
¼ cup corn oil
Vegetable oil spray
4 limes

Trim off the root ends and all but about 4 inches of the greens from the onions. Transfer the onions to a large bowl, add cold water to cover, and let soak for about 3 minutes. Stir gently to remove any sand or other grit, then lift out the onions.

In a stockpot, bring the water to a boil over high heat. Add 1 tablespoon salt and the onions and blanch for about 1 minute. Drain into a colander and place under cold running water until cool. Dry on paper towels.

In a bowl, toss the onions with the oil and 1 teaspoon salt, coating the onions evenly.

Prepare a medium-hot fire in a charcoal or gas grill. Before igniting the grill, lightly coat the grill grid with vegetable oil spray to prevent sticking. Grill the onions, turning them often so that they cook evenly, for about 5 minutes, or until they can be easily pierced with a fork.

Transfer the onions to a platter. Halve 1 lime and squeeze the juice over the onions, then sprinkle the onions with salt. Slice the remaining 3 limes and use to garnish the platter. Serve immediately.

COOK'S NOTE: *To cook the spring onions in the oven, preheat the oven to 375°F. After tossing the onions with the oil and salt, spread them on a rimmed baking sheet and bake, turning once, for about 15 minutes, or until lightly browned. Slide the baking sheet under the broiler and broil for about 2 minutes to brown further. Serve as directed.*

THIS IS A SIMPLE RECIPE, typical of how Mexicans like to prepare the small, red new potatoes farmers harvest twice a year. Adding *rajas*, or strips of poblano chiles, to the roasting pan imparts a smoky zing to the potatoes and onions. We serve the potatoes with egg dishes for brunch, but they also make a wonderful *antojito* served as is.

new potatoes roasted with poblano chiles
PAPAS POBLANAS

SERVES 6

4 cups water
Kosher salt and freshly ground black pepper
1½ pounds (about 18) small new potatoes
¼ cup olive oil
1 onion, cut into ½-inch-thick slices
3 poblano chiles, seeded, membranes removed, and cut lengthwise into ½-inch-wide strips

In a stockpot, bring the water to a boil over high heat. Add 1 tablespoon salt and the potatoes and let the water return to a boil. Cook for about 20 minutes, or until they can be easily pierced with a fork. Drain and set aside to cool.

In a sauté pan, heat the oil over medium heat. Add the onion and sauté for about 5 minutes, or until translucent and golden yellow. Lower the heat if necessary to prevent scorching, or the onion will taste bitter. Using a slotted spoon, transfer the onion to a bowl.

Return the sauté pan to medium-high heat, add the chile strips, and sauté for about 5 minutes, or until soft. Add to the onion and toss together.

Preheat the oven to 375°F. Slice the potatoes in half and add them to the onion and chile strips. Season with salt and pepper. (This dish can be made up to this point a day ahead and finished in the oven just before serving.)

Transfer the potato mixture to a roasting pan, and spread the potatoes in a single layer. Roast for about 15 minutes, or until the edges of the vegetables are slightly crispy and heated through. Serve immediately.

LA ESTRELLA

CORN

In Mexico, nearly everyone grows a *milpa*, or cornfield. In the cities, this is usually just a patch in a small garden or even on a rooftop. Every year at La Palapa on Saint Mark's Place, we cultivate a modest *milpa* in front of the restaurant. Our neighbors like seeing a little of the country in their urban landscape.

According to legend, the first humans were formed from corn *masa* (dough). The ancient Mayans originated the processing of corn kernels with limestone, which softened the grain for making *masa* and added calcium to their diet. This innovation was important for the growth and development of the complex societies and sophisticated cities of the time, ensuring not only a class of strong soldiers but also of remarkable astronomers, architects, cultivators, poets, and priests. Even then, a meal of beans, a chile salsa, and tortillas made from corn *masa* was recognized as nutritious—rich in protein, vitamins, and carbohydrates.

Today, Mexican cooks use corn *masa* to create dozens of tasty *antojitos* based on the tortilla. But even though tortillas, like pasta, are all made from the same basic dough, how they are shaped determines their nomenclature and, more important, their filling. The term *tortillas* alone refers to the flat, round, pliable corn cakes served at Mexican meals. They are wrapped around almost every tasty bite at the table, and sometimes the *masa* used to make them is flavored and tinted: nopal cactus paddles for green dough, bananas for yellow, and achiote paste for red. Cousins of the flat tortilla, all of them made with corn *masa* as well, include open-faced, round and oval "boats" called *sopes* and *chalupas*, filled with chorizo or beans; flat *huaraches* and *tlayudas*, topped with a hot salsa and *queso fresco* or shredded pork *asiento*; and pockets called quesadillas, *gorditas*, *doraditas*, and *tlacoyos*, stuffed with chile-spiked chicken, epazote-scented beans, and fresh cheeses.

HOW TO WARM CORN OR FLOUR TORTILLAS

Tortillas taste best when served warm. They are also more supple, making it easier to wrap them around a filling. In Mexico, they are brought to the table in a shallow, lidded dish or basket that traps the heat. Here are two methods for warming tortillas and a tip on how to keep them warm:

▸ Put several tortillas in a single layer on a griddle or in a dry nonstick skillet set over medium-low heat. Heat them for about 30 seconds and then turn them, without overlapping, so they warm on both sides and do not burn.

▸ To warm more than a few tortillas at a time, stack 10 or 12 together and wrap them in a damp paper towel. Microwave the paper-wrapped package on high power for 30 seconds. Unwrap the package very carefully—the steam is hot. Shuffle the order of the stacked tortillas, putting those in the center at the top or bottom, rewrap, and microwave for 15 seconds longer.

▸ If you want to warm a large number of tortillas ahead of time, heat them as directed above, arrange them in a stack of 15 or 20 in a clean cloth napkin or kitchen towel, and then wrap the entire package tightly in aluminum foil. The tortillas will stay warm for up to an hour.

Corn is also used to make *atole*, a porridgelike drink made by mixing the *masa* with milk or water and with chocolate, nuts, or fruits such as strawberries or guavas. Of course, every part of the corn plant is put to use in the Mexican kitchen. The kernels are transformed into hominy and used in hearty soups called *pozoles*. The ears are steamed and sprinkled with *queso añejo* and *piquín* chile powder. The husks are wrapped around tamales and are sometimes used as receptacles for guacamole and other salsas. Mexicans also prize *huitlacoche*, a fungus that grows on corn kernels and imparts a flavor that marries mushrooms and corn in each mouthful.

> The Aztecs called corn *teocintle*, or "food of the gods."

CHILES

Chiles show up everywhere in Mexican cooking. Their heat, due to the naturally occurring capsaicin compound, provides spicy brilliance to a wide array of dishes. Understanding chiles is key to good Mexican cooking, and although you could easily devote a lifetime to the study of the hundreds of chile varieties grown worldwide, it is not nearly as time-consuming to learn what you need to know to cook Mexican dishes successfully.

Fresh chiles are harvested either green and unripe or red (or sometimes orange or yellow) and ripe. Once they are ripe, they have some sweetness, although a hot chile will be just as hot when it is red as when it is green. Dried chiles are simply fresh chiles allowed to air-dry so their moisture evaporates and their skins wrinkle. Some are then smoked, as well. Typically, ripe red chiles are dried, although some green chiles are also dried. When chiles are dried, they are usually assigned a new name. For example, the fresh poblano is called an ancho chile when dried.

Salsas, which include not only the familiar table condiments but also moles and adobos, are made from all types of chiles. Because not all chiles are hot, not all salsas are hot. On the contrary, many are pleasantly mild. Knowing how to pair salsas and food is an art that the best Mexican cooks master with grace and creativity. How Mexican home cooks use salsas depends on where they live. In central Mexico, for example, meats are cooked in chile-paste marinades known as adobos and moles, both of which infuse the meat with spiciness that is mellowed by eating the dishes with tortillas. In the Yucatán, mild dishes are paired with fiery salsas made with habanero chiles.

Aztec priests equated the heat of the chile with spiritual strength. Although no one subscribes to this theory now, chiles are still used for a number of ceremonial rituals. We both feel blessed to have been part of a *limpia*, or spiritual cleansing, performed by Doña Nico, a friend and wonderful cook, at the Mexico City home of artist Helen Escobedo. For the cleansing, we brought a pair of perfect *pasilla* chiles, which Doña Nico rubbed on us to give us strength. The *limpia* was conducted beneath one of Escobedo's paintings, in which she had used mole as pigment. Talk about symbiosis!

Fresh Chiles

Most chiles are harvested with the stems on, which keeps them fresh longer. When buying chiles, select firm specimens with their stems intact and with smooth skin free of breaks. Store them in a loosely closed plastic bag in the crisper of the refrigerator, where they should keep for about 2 weeks, and rinse them with cool running water just before using. If they have been waxed, you may want to use a food-safe soap to cleanse them.

How to Peel Fresh Chiles

Some fresh chiles, particularly poblanos and jalapeños, are sometimes peeled to remove their naturally thick skin. To peel them, you must roast them first, which loosens the skin so you can rub it off. The flesh, which is not cooked through, can then be used for *rajas* (chile strips) or the whole chile can be stuffed.

1. Wash and dry the chiles, then roast them over a gas flame on the stove top, in the broiler, or on a grill. To roast over a gas flame, grasp a chile with tongs and hold it over the flame until it blisters, rotating it as needed to char and blister it evenly on all sides. To roast in a broiler, arrange the chiles on a rimmed baking sheet lined with aluminum foil, place in the broiler about 4 inches from the heat source, and broil, turning as needed, until evenly charred and blistered on all sides. To roast on a grill, arrange the chiles directly over a medium-hot fire and grill, again turning as needed to char and blister evenly. The timing will vary depending on the intensity of the heat and method, but plan on 10 to 15 minutes.

2. Once blackened, put the chiles in a bowl and cover with plastic wrap or a damp kitchen towel. Let the chiles steam for about 15 minutes.

3. Use your fingers or a small knife to rub or peel off the skin. It should come off easily. Don't worry if a few flecks of blackened skin remain. The dish will be just as authentic. And don't hold the chiles under running water as you peel them. Their flesh will absorb the water, which will diminish their flavor.

4. Be careful when you cut the chiles. They may still be filled with hot steam. Also, take care when handling them, as the capsaicin can burn your eyes and skin.

5. Peeled roasted chiles will keep in a lidded container in the refrigerator for up to 5 days, but they do not freeze well.

Habanero chiles are commonly found in dishes from the Yucatán and are considered one of the world's hottest chiles. Lantern shaped and about 2 inches long, they can be green, yellow, or light orange and are nearly always sold fresh. You can also find them dried and ground into powder in Mexican markets and in other stores specializing in Latin food.

Jalapeño chiles are thick fleshed and about 3 inches long. They are bright green before they ripen, which is how they are usually sold. When they ripen, they turn bright red and still maintain their vibrant, unmistakable kick. Pickled jalapeños, sold in jars and cans, are usually labeled *jalapeños en escabeche*. They are often pickled with vegetables, such as onions, carrots, and cauliflower, which, along with the pickling brine, concentrate the spiciness of the chile.

Piquín **chiles** grow on a vine and are small, about ½ inch long. They are picked both green and red. Red, ripe chiles taste delightfully fruity and are usually dried and ground to make *piquín* chile powder, which is commonly used to season fruits and vegetables. At La Palapa, we mix the chile powder in the salt we use to rim glasses for our margaritas.

Poblano chiles, which are about 5 inches long, have tough skins, so they are generally roasted and then peeled. This gives them a distinct smokiness that plays nicely with their heat, which can vary from mild to fairly hot. Because of their meatiness, poblanos are commonly cut into strips known as *rajas*. They are also typically used for stuffing.

Serrano chiles are small, slim, and similar to jalapeños in flavor, heat intensity, and size. At La Palapa, we mostly use them green. Red, ripe serranos, which are a little sweet, are often used in salsas.

Dried Chiles

Dried chiles should be shiny and a little flexible—they must never be so dry that they crumble in your fingers—and have their stems intact. They should be whole, too. Buy them in small quantities; you will never use a large amount before they become brittle and a little tired. (If you cannot find the chiles you need at a local market, look for them online at www.mexgrocer.com or other sites selling Mexican ingredients.) Store them in airtight containers in a dry place, away from direct sunlight. Just before you use them, wipe them clean with a damp cloth.

Pure chile powder is made by finely grinding dried chiles. Buy the powder only if it has an intense color and rich aroma. Again, buy in small amounts and store in an airtight container in a dry place, away from direct sunlight.

How to Make a Dried Chile Paste

Dried chiles are typically softened and then ground in a blender or food processor into a paste for making adobos and other salsas. These chile pastes freeze well and can be kept on hand to make a quick and rich *salsa de chiles secos.*

1. Wipe the dried chiles with a damp cloth. Remove the stems and shake out the seeds and membranes, or ribs. Reserve the seeds and membranes for adding to salsas to crank up the heat. Toast the chiles lightly in a heavy, dry skillet or griddle over medium heat for 30 seconds to 1 minute, or until they soften and plump up.

2. Put the chiles in a glass or other nonreactive bowl. Add hot water to cover and let soak for about 20 minutes and for no more than 40 minutes. Remove the chiles from the water—they should be soft and pliable—and reserve the soaking water.

3. Transfer the chiles to a blender or food processor and process until smooth, using some of the soaking water as needed to achieve a smooth puree. Push the puree through a coarse-mesh sieve.

4. Use at once or refrigerate in a resealable plastic bag or small, covered bowl for up to 1 week. For longer storage, put the paste in a freezer bag, seal tightly, and freeze for up to 1 month.

Ancho chiles are dried green poblano chiles. When they dry, they wrinkle and turn reddish brown and their flavor is mellow and sweet, with just a touch of heat.

Árbol **chiles** are paper-thin and long and add a lot of spice to dishes, particularly salsas. They can be used whole or ground and often are added to a mild salsa to heat it up.

Cascabel **chiles** are small and round, about 2 inches in diameter, and are usually harvested when ripe and then dried. They are sweet, and their heat may be mild or medium. The name comes from the Spanish word for "rattle," probably because you can hear the seeds rattle around when you shake the chiles.

Chipotle chiles are dried, smoked ripe jalapeño chiles. When packed in a can of adobo, a tomato-based sauce, they are called *chipotles en adobo*. Many recipes call for the chiles and the sauce, either together or separately. Both are spicy.

Guajillo **chiles** are long, thin, and bright orange-red. When their seeds are used with the chile, the chile is very spicy. But if the seeds and membranes are removed, it is only mildly hot, though still tangy.

Morita **chiles** are named "little berry" because they are small and brown. These smoked chiles are intensely spicy and similar to chipotles, but with less smokiness and a little less heat.

Mulato **chiles** are poblano chiles allowed to ripen to a deep purple and then dried, turning nearly black. They are both sweet and slightly bitter, with medium fire.

Pasilla **chiles**, which are long, narrow, and dark brown, are dried *chilaca* chiles. Similar in flavor to the more popular ancho, *pasilla*s are most often used with other dried chiles in traditional moles. *Pasilla* means "raisin," which is a good indication of how sweet this chile can be. The smaller *pasilla* chile from Oaxaca is usually smoked before it is added to salsas and moles.

> *La mejor salsa es el apetito.*
>
> Appetite is the best sauce.
>
> —JUAN BENITO DÍAZ DE GAMARRA

SALSAS

Salsas are on the dinner table of every home in Mexico. This may explain why salsas have the reputation of being as different from one another as the cooks are who make them. Despite this legacy, there are three basic types: *salsa fresca* (made with fresh ingredients), *salsa macha* (made with charred, roasted ingredients), and *salsa de chiles secos* (made with dried chiles).

Salsas frescas are served at room temperature or chilled. Ideally made with seasonal ingredients, they are refreshing and piquant and can vary from savory to sweet and fruity. These salsas typically entice your taste buds with sweet, sour, spicy, and salty flavors all at once.

Salsas machas are made from charred, roasted, or partially cooked foods that are roughly chopped or mashed before they are stirred together. These rustic salsas are generally quite spicy, in part because the flavors of the chiles intensify when the chiles are charred. *Salsas machas* are a good choice when a spicy condiment is desired.

Salsas de chiles secos are made from toasting and then soaking dried chiles. The fruitiness of the dried chiles combines well with sweet notes such as cinnamon and saffron. The salsas can be hot and fiery or mild and understated, depending on the amount of seeds incorporated into the salsa. They are served warm as sauces for fish, grilled meats, and cheese, or at room temperature as condiments for tacos and quesadillas.

AROMATICS

Whenever we visit Mexico, one of our favorite outings is to walk through a *mercado* and let the aromatic spices and herbs of the Mexican pantry hijack our senses: the soft, sweet aroma of cinnamon bark mixing with the bite of whole cumin seeds and the dark green anise scent of avocado leaves; black pepper mingling with the pungent fragrance of allspice, cloves, and pumpkin seeds; cones of *piloncillo* (unrefined sugar) sparring with the tang of tamarind pods. It is easy to understand why Mexicans call their spices *olores*, or "aromas." Indeed, it is almost impossible to buy only what is on our shopping list. Instead, we find ourselves dreaming, perhaps, of a new mole with the shiny sesame seeds and the papery raw peanuts we see, or of a new salsa with the cumin and anise that beckon.

At La Palapa, we keep these aromatics on hand, and when we think about new *antojitos* to create, we usually begin by tasting and smelling these fragrant ingredients. They never fail to both inspire us and transport us back to our trip through the *mercado*.

Spices and Seeds

Achiote paste, a fragrant mixture of annatto seeds, garlic, oregano, cumin, cinnamon, pepper, and cloves, is a popular seasoning for marinades and sauces in the Yucatán.

Aniseeds are originally from the Middle East and were enthusiastically adopted by Mexican cooks as a substitute for *hoja santa* and, on occasion, avocado leaves. Aniseeds flavor the *masa* used for making *gorditas*.

Annatto seeds—tiny, rock-hard, brick red seeds from the South American annatto tree—are what give a lot of Mexican food an orange tint. The seeds have a slightly musty flavor. When ground and combined with other ingredients, they are transformed into achiote paste.

Black peppercorns are the familiar dried, tiny wrinkled berries of the pepper tree. Mexican cooks rely on their spicy heat in most cooked dishes.

Cinnamon comes in two types, soft bark and hard bark. Mexican cooks prefer the soft, or loose, bark variety from a a tree grown only in Sri Lanka. It has a slightly smoky, delicate flavor and is thought to be the "true cinnamon." If you cannot find Mexican cinnamon, use the best cinnamon you can find.

Cloves, the buds of a tree of Indonesian origin, have a strong, astringent aroma. They are always used judiciously, as their flavor, which is both spicy and sweet, can be intensely penetrating, whether in a sweet or savory dish.

Coriander seeds are the dried seeds of the cilantro plant, but they don't mimic the flavor of the leafy herb. They are found primarily in moles and adobos, particularly in central Mexico.

Cumin seeds are tiny but packed with a distinctive flavor, and a little of this rich-tasting spice goes a long way. If a recipe calls for ground cumin, toast the seeds and grind them yourself in a spice grinder for the best

flavor and aroma. This spice will easily overtake a dish, so use sparingly.

Pepitas are the green seeds of pumpkins, which are native to Mexico. They show up in sauces, salads, and moles and as a snack food. *Pipián* is a pumpkin seed sauce made with dried red or green chiles or with fresh green chiles. At La Palapa, we serve fish with *pipián*.

Saffron is the stigma of a crocus flower and was introduced to Mexico by the Spanish. Although native to Asia, it is grown and widely used in Spain and, not surprisingly, turns up in Mexican recipes of Spanish origin.

Dried and Fresh Herbs

Avocado leaves, which are used fresh and dried, are about 7 inches long and 3 inches across. The leaves used in Mexican cooking are from a tree common in Mexico, rather than the popular Hass tree well known in the United States. The best leaves are picked from large trees and have an aniselike, herby aroma and flavor. In some recipes, the leaves are lightly toasted, then ground and cooked with other ingredients. Bay leaves are a common substitute, and like bay leaves, when used whole, they are removed from a dish after cooking. Fresh leaves are difficult to find in U.S. markets, so fresh or dried leaves can be used in our recipes.

Bay leaves, which are used fresh and dried, are the long, oval leaves of the Mediterranean laurel tree and are most commonly used whole to flavor sauces and soups. It is important to remove bay leaves from a dish after it has finished cooking because their sharp flavor can infuse it as it sits. In *mercados*, bay leaves are often sold fresh in bunches with thyme and marjoram as *hierbas de olor*, or "aromatic herbs." Fresh bay leaves are also available in the United States and can be used in the same way as dried leaves.

Cilantro, which is used fresh, was brought to Mexico by the Spanish, where it was enthusiastically embraced. Its bright, pungent flavor arouses passionate feelings: people either love it or hate it. Cilantro, sometimes labeled Chinese parsley or fresh coriander, is used in fresh salsas and as a garnish on many *antojitos*. It is rarely, if ever, sold dried.

Epazote, which is used fresh, grows wild in many areas of North America. In Mexican cuisine, it is used in quesadillas and is added to the cooking pot with beans, mushrooms, and corn. When raw, epazote has a pungent, strong, earthy smell, which mellows considerably when cooked, becoming reminiscent of a mixture of sage and parsley.

Hoja santa, which is used fresh and dried, is a large, soft leaf with a taste that balances green herbaceousness with a touch of anise. Mexican cooks wrap this "holy leaf" around tamales and use it in quesadillas. Its flavor is very strong when fresh. When dried, the flavor diminishes, which is why dried *hoja santa* is considered inferior.

Oregano, which is used fresh or dried, is one of the most popular dried herbs in Mexican cooking. It has mild overtones of mint, and when dried is favored for

broths, moles, adobos, and other salsas and is an essential ingredient in all *escabeches* (pickles). It is far less frequently used fresh but does show up from time to time. Although native to Asia and Europe, four different regional varieties are grown in Mexico.

Thyme, which is used fresh or dried, is found in marinades for meats and in dishes of Spanish origin.

Other Flavorings

Adobo is a sweet-tart Mexican barbecue sauce or chile paste. It can be a marinade or rub and often doubles as a salsa.

Chocolate is indigenous to Mexico. When the pods of the cacao tree are harvested, the seeds are dried, toasted, and ground. The Aztecs combined the ground pods with vanilla and chile and added the mixture to water to make a frothy drink. Even today the husks of the cacao pods are toasted and added to moles and other salsas. Chocolate is also an integral part of black and red moles. Mexican hot chocolate is usually scented with cinnamon.

Piloncillo is unrefined sugar formed into cones. The cones, which have a distinctive molasses flavor, are grated for making sweet syrups and for adding to *café de olla*, flavored with cloves, orange, and cinnamon.

Tamarind pulp is derived from tamarind trees, which produce dried, brown seedpods filled with a sticky sweet-sour pulp that cushions the seeds. In Mexico, the pulp is combined with salt, chile, and sugar to make candied snacks. The pulp is also softened, strained, and mixed with water to make a refreshing *agua fresca*. At La Palapa, we add it to margaritas, as well.

Vanilla beans are the fruit of the vanilla orchid, which is indigenous to Mexico. In fact, it can be said that any dessert made with chocolate or vanilla owes a debt to Mexico.

CHEESES

Many regions in Mexico produce cheese, both fresh and aged, made from the milk of cows, sheep, or goats, or a combination, and local cooks use them for stuffing chiles or quesadillas, for melting into rich *fundidos* (fondues), and for sprinkling on all kinds of spicy *antojitos* to temper their heat. Nowadays, authentic Mexican cheeses can be found in many supermarkets in the United States. Here are the cheeses used in this book:

Queso añejo, a dry, aged cow's milk cheese prized for its salty bite, is usually combined with other cheeses. We use it in our three-cheese quesadillas (page 17) and our César salad (page 112). As it ages, it becomes saltier and drier until it is so hard it is no longer a melting cheese. At this point, it is known as *queso Cotija* (see below). Both cheeses can be used as a salty garnish for *antojitos*.

Queso Chihuahua, a tangy, pale yellow melting cheese, was first produced by the Mennonites who emigrated to the state of Chihuahua in northern Mexico. Made from cow's milk, it is used for quesadillas (page 17) and many other dishes.

Queso Cotija is a long-aged *queso añejo*, named after the town in Michoacán in which it was first made.

Queso fresco, a fresh cow's milk cheese, is white and slightly salty, with a texture similar to that of farmer cheese. At La Palapa, we make our own *queso fresco*, using up to 80 gallons of pasteurized, organic whole milk every week.

Queso manchego is a mild, semisoft cow's milk cheese. An excellent melting cheese, it is named after the famous Spanish semihard sheep's milk cheese.

Queso Oaxaca is a fresh, whole-milk string cheese used in quesadillas and *queso fundido* in central Mexico. It is also eaten as is as a *botana* (snack).

OUR SOUR MIX is on the tart side, so if you prefer a sweeter mix, add more sugar. This is the mixer used for margaritas and other classic cocktails, such as a whiskey sour, a Tom Collins, or a Long Island iced tea.

sour mix

JARABE AGRIO

MAKES ABOUT 8 CUPS

- 4 cups water
- ¾ cup sugar
- 4 cups store-bought or freshly squeezed lime juice

In a saucepan, bring the water and sugar to a boil over medium-high heat, stirring several times to dissolve the sugar. Let the syrup boil for about 3 minutes, or until the sugar is thoroughly dissolved and the syrup is clear. Remove from the heat and allow to cool completely. Add the lime juice a little at a time, stirring constantly. Transfer the mix to a jar with a tight-fitting lid and refrigerate for up to 5 days.

WE USE THIS CHILE SALT for margaritas and beer cocktails. We even sprinkle it on our food. You can make the salt as spicy as you want, although we recommend adding the chile powder a little at a time. It's hot!

piquín chile salt

SAL DE CHILE PIQUÍN

MAKES ¼ CUP

- 3 tablespoons kosher salt
- About 1 tablespoon piquín chile powder

In a small bowl, mix together the salt and chile powder.

Use immediately, or transfer to a small jar with a tight-fitting lid and store at room temperature.

MEXICAN COOKS have adopted the French crêpe, filling it with everything from *huitlacoche* to plantains and *cajeta* (goat's milk caramel).

crêpes

CREPAS

MAKES ABOUT 20 CRÊPES

2 cups whole milk
2 large eggs
4 large egg yolks
2 tablespoons sugar
1 teaspoon kosher salt
1½ cups all-purpose flour
About 4 tablespoons unsalted butter

In a bowl, using an electric mixer, mix together the milk, eggs, egg yolks, sugar, and salt until blended. Slowly add the flour, beating continuously just until smooth. A few small lumps of flour are okay. Let the batter rest for about 10 minutes.

In a nonstick 8-inch skillet, melt about 1 teaspoon of the butter over medium heat. Drop 2 tablespoons of the batter onto the pan and swirl the pan to spread the batter in a paper-thin layer over the bottom. Cook for about 30 seconds, or until the first side is lightly browned. Then turn the crêpe with a rubber spatula and cook for about 15 seconds longer to brown the second side. Transfer the crêpe to a plate.

Repeat until you have used all of the batter, adding more butter to the pan as needed. You should have about 20 crêpes. The first few might not be perfect and can be discarded. As each crêpe is cooked, stack it on top of the last one on the plate. If not using immediately, let the crêpes cool completely, cover the stack tightly with plastic wrap, and refrigerate for up to 1 week. If when you are ready to use them some have dried out, use only the pliable ones and discard the others.

MEXICAN *CREMA* IS USED in many dishes to complement and soften the spicy bite of chiles. It also adds a savory note to sweet dishes, such as fried plantains, and splendidly enriches soups. We like it on its own as a dip for *totopos* (page 15).

You can purchase *crema* in Mexican markets and some supermarkets, but it is easy to make at home. We use a tablespoon of a previous batch as the starter, or culture, for the next batch. For the home cook, this is not usually practical, unless you plan to use *crema* on an almost daily basis. Of course, once you try this, you may decide you always want it in your refrigerator.

mexican sour cream

CREMA MEXICANA

MAKES ABOUT 3 CUPS

2 cups sour cream
1 cup heavy cream
1 teaspoon kosher salt

In a nonreactive bowl, whisk together the sour cream and heavy cream. Whisk in the salt. Set aside at room temperature for about 20 minutes.

Whisk again, taste, and add more salt, if needed. Cover and refrigerate for up to 8 hours. The *crema* will taste best if allowed to mellow for the entire 8 hours, though you can serve it immediately. It will keep, well covered, in the refrigerator for up to 4 days.

Chalupas, boatlike *antojitos* made from corn *masa*, vary in shape—flat, oval, round, canoe shaped—and size, depending on the region. We make them round, which is how they are made in the colonial city of Puebla. When they are larger, about 4 inches across, they are known as *sopes*, and when they are large ovals, about 8 inches long, they are *huaraches*, named after the traditional Mexican sandals. Mexican cooks are full of whimsy and may even make them heart shaped for a festive San Valentín dish.

In every form or size, they are perfect vessels for all kinds of fillings, from fish, chorizo, and cheese to vegetables and poultry.

corn masa boats

CHALUPAS

MAKES 12 CHALUPAS

- 1 generous cup masa harina, plus additional if needed
- ¼ teaspoon kosher salt
- 1 cup warm water
- Corn oil, for frying

In a large bowl, stir together the *masa harina* and salt. Slowly add the water, working it into the flour with your hands to form a dough. Knead the dough for 3 to 5 minutes, or until moist and smooth but not sticky. If the dough seems too dry, moisten your hands with water and knead in the dampness. If it seems too wet, add more flour, 1 tablespoon at a time, and knead until moist and smooth.

Divide the dough into 12 equal balls. Form each ball into a disk about ½ inch thick.

Heat a griddle or cast-iron skillet over medium-high heat. Working in batches, place the disks on the hot pan and cook, turning once, for about 3 minutes on each side, or until a crust forms on both sides. As you remove the disks from the pan, pinch the edge of each one to create a rim about ⅓ inch high. Pinch the center three times to lift and thin the middle of each *chalupa*.

Set the *chalupas* on a plate to cool completely, then cover with plastic wrap until ready to use.

In a skillet, pour the oil to a depth of about ½ inch and heat over medium-high heat until a small piece of the dough dropped into the oil sizzles on contact. Gently fry the *chalupas*, turning once, for about 2 minutes on each side, or until crisp and lightly golden. Do not brown them or they will toughen. Carefully lift them from the oil, drain on paper towels, and fill immediately.

Or, let the *chalupas* cool completely, wrap tightly in plastic wrap, and store in an airtight, rigid container at room temperature for up to 3 days. Then, just before serving, reheat in a dry skillet or griddle over medium heat, turning as needed, or wrap them, a few at a time, in a paper towel and reheat in a microwave oven on high power for 15 to 30 seconds.

WE SERVE THIS VERSATILE CHORIZO in *chalupas*, quesadillas, and *fundidos*, and scrambled in *huevos choriqueso*. It is inspired by the sausage we learned to make from Domingo Torres, our head chef, who learned it from his mother, Crispina. It is so delicious, we sauté it after allowing it to mellow for only a few hours in the refrigerator. Who can wait longer?

guajillo-spiked pork chorizo
CHORIZO CASERO

MAKES ABOUT 1½ POUNDS

- 3 árbol chiles
- 7 guajillo chiles
- ½ cup coarsely chopped onion
- 1 clove garlic, chopped
- 1 bay leaf
- ½ cup distilled white vinegar
- 1 tablespoon kosher salt
- 2 teaspoons ground cumin
- 2 teaspoons dried Mexican oregano
- 1½ teaspoons ground cloves
- 1 teaspoon freshly ground black pepper
- 1 pound ground pork

In a nonreactive bowl or shallow dish, layer the chiles, onion, and garlic. Add the bay leaf. Pour in the vinegar and cover the dish tightly with plastic wrap. Set aside at room temperature for 1 hour.

Remove and discard the bay leaf. Transfer the chile-vinegar mixture to a blender and process to form a rough paste. If the paste is too thick to process easily, thin it by adding water, 1 tablespoon at a time.

In a bowl, thoroughly mix together the chile paste, salt, cumin, oregano, cloves, and pepper. Add the pork and mix until the paste and spices are evenly distributed.

To test for seasoning, in a nonstick skillet set over medium heat, cook about ½ teaspoon of the pork mixture. Taste the cooked sausage and add more salt to the raw mixture, if necessary. Repeat until the sausage is seasoned as you like it.

Put the raw sausage meat in a container with a tight-fitting lid and refrigerate for at least 12 hours or up to 5 days. If you are keeping it longer than 5 days, transfer it to a resealable plastic freezer bag and freeze for up to 2 months.

MOLES ARE TIME-CONSUMING to prepare, but no other Mexican sauce can match them in complexity and depth of flavor, so they are worth the effort. This is our recipe for a lightly spiced Oaxacan black mole, which often turns up at weddings and other celebrations, but is also a welcome sight on any dinner table. Traditionally, it is served with chicken or with turkey, Mexico's indigenous fowl, but it dresses up other dishes, too, such as crêpes filled with plantains (page 120) or duck (page 73).

oaxaca-style black mole

MOLE NEGRO OAXAQUEÑO

MAKES ABOUT 4 QUARTS

6 to 7 mulato chiles

5 guajillo chiles

4 pasilla chiles

4 ancho chiles

3 or 4 chipotle chiles, dried or canned

1 onion, quartered

½ head garlic, cloves separated and peeled

¼ cup blanched almonds

2 tablespoons raw peanuts

1 tablespoon ground Mexican cinnamon

5 black peppercorns

5 whole cloves

5 tablespoons high-quality lard or vegetable shortening

3 tablespoons raisins

1 thick slice egg bread, such as brioche

1 ripe plantain with black skin, peeled and cut into ½-inch-thick slices

½ cup sesame seeds

5 pecan halves

6 plum tomatoes, cored and quartered

6 tomatillos, husks removed, cored, and quartered

1 teaspoon dried thyme

1 teaspoon dried Mexican oregano

7 to 8 cups low-sodium chicken broth

4½ ounces Mexican chocolate or bittersweet chocolate, broken into pieces

2 dried avocado leaves, toasted and ground, or pinch of ground fennel seeds

Kosher salt

Stem all the chiles, scrape out and reserve the seeds, and remove and discard the membranes. In a heavy skillet, toast the chiles over medium heat, turning as needed, for 30 seconds to 1 minute, or until they soften and plump up. Transfer the chiles to a bowl, add hot water to cover, and let stand for about 30 minutes. Transfer the chiles to a food processor or blender with a few tablespoons of the soaking water and process until a paste forms. Push the paste through a coarse-mesh sieve into a nonreactive bowl.

In the same skillet, grill the onion and garlic over medium-high heat, turning as needed, for about 5 minutes, or until darkened on all sides but not charred. Set aside on a plate.

Using the same skillet, toast the almonds, peanuts, cinnamon, peppercorns, and cloves for about 2 minutes, or just until the nuts darken a shade and the mixture is fragrant. Transfer to a spice grinder or mini food processor and grind to a powder. Set aside.

Spread the reserved chile seeds in the same skillet and toast over medium-high heat, shaking the pan to encourage even blackening, for about 30 seconds, or until blackened. Transfer to a small bowl, cover with cold water, and let soak for about 10 minutes. Drain and then grind in the spice grinder. Add to the chile paste.

In the same skillet, heat 3 tablespoons of the lard over medium-high heat. Add the raisins and fry for about 3 minutes, or until plump. Using a slotted spoon, transfer to a small bowl.

Add the bread slice to the lard in the skillet and toast over medium-high heat for about 1 minute on each side, or until golden brown. Transfer to a plate, again leaving the lard in the skillet.

Put the plantain slices in the skillet over medium-high heat and cook, turning as needed, for about 5 minutes, or until well browned on both sides. Set aside with the bread.

Pour off the fat from the skillet, wipe dry with a paper towel, and return to medium heat. Add the sesame seeds and heat for 1 to 2 minutes, or until lightly browned. Remove from the pan. Add the pecans to the skillet and toast for 1 to 2 minutes, or until the nuts darken a shade and are fragrant. Remove from the pan and let cool.

When the raisins, bread, plantains, sesame seeds, and pecans are cool, grind them together in the food processor. Set aside.

Wipe out the skillet with a paper towel. Put the tomatoes, tomatillos, thyme, and oregano in the skillet over medium-high heat and cook, stirring, for about 10 minutes, or until the juices from the tomatoes and tomatillos are released and then reduce to almost nothing. Transfer the mixture to the food processor and puree until smooth. Remove and set aside.

Working in batches, add the raisin-bread mixture, onion, and garlic to the food processor and process until the consistency of smooth peanut butter, adding up to 1 cup of the broth to achieve the desired consistency.

In a nonreactive, 4-quart stockpot, heat the remaining 2 tablespoons lard over medium-high heat just until it begins to smoke. Add the chile paste, reduce the heat to medium, and cook, stirring constantly, for 15 to 20 minutes, or until the paste stiffens a little and resembles tomato paste.

CONTINUED▶

MORE ON MOLES

The state of Oaxaca is known for its moles, including *amarillo, coloradito, chichilo negro, manchamanteles, verde*, and, the most famous of all, *mole negro*. But the sister superior of the Santa Rosa Convent in Puebla, in the Mexican state of the same name, is credited with making the first mole, reportedly as a surprise for the bishop who had a convent built for her order.

Many moles include more than two dozen ingredients, but there are traditionally three main components: chiles; nuts, seeds, and often chocolate; and spices. A common misconception is that every mole includes chocolate, and while many do, it is not found in all of them. A second misconception is that *mole negro* gets its name from the addition of chocolate. Although it does call for chocolate, it is actually named for the chocolate-colored dried chiles that impart both their robust flavor and their bold color. This is true of all moles: their color derives from the chiles they contain. For example, *mole rojo* is made with red chiles and *mole amarillo* is made with yellow chiles.

Add the tomato puree and cook for about 5 minutes, stirring constantly, until the consistency of tomato paste. Add the ground almond mixture and stir well. Stir in 1 cup of the broth and bring to a boil. Reduce the heat and simmer, stirring occasionally, for about 5 minutes, or until the broth evaporates. Add 1 more cup of the broth and the chocolate and stir until the chocolate melts.

Add the avocado leaves, season with salt, and simmer gently for about 1 hour. As the mole simmers, stir in as much of the remaining 5 cups broth as needed to create a mixture with the consistency of a gravy. Watch the mole carefully and stir often to avoid scorching.

Remove from the heat and use as directed in individual recipes. Or, let cool, cover, and refrigerate for up to 2 weeks.

COOK'S NOTE: *In Mexico, it is traditional to stew meats directly in mole. Chicken, turkey, and pork are especially tasty preapred in this black mole. In a saucepan or stockpot, sear cubes of the meat in a little oil until browned, then add the mole and simmer, stirring often to prevent scorching, until the meat is cooked through.*

RICE IS A STAPLE of the Mexican table, and when a pinch of saffron is added at the end of cooking, it is especially prized. Mexican home cooks prepare rice daily, and it is important to know how to cook it so that it turns out light and fluffy.

saffron rice
ARROZ AL AZAFRÁN

MAKES ABOUT 3 CUPS; SERVES 6

2 cups water
2 tablespoons unsalted butter
1 teaspoon kosher salt
Freshly ground black pepper
1 cup long-grain white rice
½ teaspoon saffron threads

In a 2-quart saucepan with a tight-fitting lid, bring the water to a boil over high heat. Add the butter and salt and season with a little pepper. When the butter melts, stir in the rice. Reduce the heat to medium-low, cover, and simmer the rice for about 25 minutes, or until all the water is absorbed. Adjust the heat as need to maintain a gentle simmer.

Remove the rice from the heat and stir in the saffron threads. Cover and set aside for about 5 minutes to give the flavor of the saffron time to bloom. Fluff the rice with a fork and serve hot.

THIS SIMPLE CHICKEN, gently simmered with aromatics and then boned, skinned, and cut into cubes or shredded by hand, is used to fill tamales (page 67) and *taquitos* (page 71), but can also be used for tacos and other popular *antojitos*.

chicken for stuffing
POLLO PARA RELLENOS

MAKES ABOUT 3 CUPS SHREDDED
OR CUBED CHICKEN

    2 large bone-in, skin-on whole chicken breasts,
        rinsed and patted dry
    1 small onion
    6 black peppercorns
    1 tablespooon kosher salt
    1 bay leaf

In a stockpot, combine the chicken breasts, onion, peppercorns, salt, bay leaf, and water to cover by about 1 inch. Bring to a boil over medium-high heat, lower the heat to medium-low, and simmer for about 45 minutes, or until the juices run clear when the meat closest to the bone is pierced with a knife tip.

Remove from the heat. Remove the chicken breasts from the broth and, when cool enough to handle, skin and bone them. Cut the meat or shred with your fingers as directed in individual recipes. Strain the broth and reserve for another use.

The chicken may be stored in a lidded container in the refrigerator for up to 5 days. The broth may be stored in the refrigerator for up to 5 days or frozen for up to 1 month.

WE USE THIS easy-to-cook but flavorful duck as a topping for tostadas (page 69) and for cradling in *sopes* (page 73), but it would also be good tucked into tacos and in other *antojitos*. To reduce the amount of fat the duck breasts release, we remove half of the skin before cooking, which still leaves plenty of fat to keep the meat juicy.

grilled duck
PATO A LA PARRILLA

MAKES ABOUT 2 CUPS SLICED DUCK

    3 (8-ounce) boneless duck breasts, rinsed and
        patted dry
    Kosher salt and freshly ground black pepper
    3 tablespoons olive oil
    2 cloves garlic, finely chopped

With a sharp knife, remove about half of the fatty skin from each duck breast: cut lengthwise down the center of the breast, cutting only through the skin, and peel away half of the skin. Season both sides of the breasts with salt and pepper, and then rub both sides with the oil and garlic. Put the breasts in a shallow container, cover, and refrigerate for 3 hours.

Heat a grill pan or skillet over medium-high heat. Add the duck breasts, skin side down, and sear for about 3 minutes, or until browned. Turn and sear for about 2 minutes longer, or until browned. Lower the heat to medium and cook for about 3 minutes, or until rare at the center when pierced with a knife.

Transfer the duck breasts to a cutting board and let rest for 10 minutes. (They will continue to cook as they rest.) Then, cut on the diagonal into slices ¼ inch thick.

The duck may be stored in a lidded container in the refrigerator for up to 3 days.

THERE IS NOTHING COMPLICATED about cooking beans, and we think a good recipe should taste homemade—never like a restaurant dish—which this one definitely does. Cook the beans slowly, and don't salt them until they are done. Let them cool completely before refrigerating them for storage. If you refrigerate warm beans, they will spoil. Serve the beans with tostadas or *chalupas*, or add them to quesadillas.

slow-cooked vegetarian pinto beans
FRIJOLES PINTOS TRADICIONALES

MAKES ABOUT 6 CUPS; SERVES 6

2 cups dried pinto beans
12 cups (3 quarts) water
3 tablespoons corn oil
½ cup chopped onion
1 cup chopped tomato
1 clove garlic, chopped
½ jalapeño chile, chopped
¼ cup chopped fresh cilantro leaves
2 teaspoons kosher salt

Rinse the beans and make sure they are free of stones and grit. Put them in a stockpot and add the water. Set over high heat and bring to a boil. Reduce the heat to medium and simmer, uncovered, for about 2½ hours, or until they are tender but not mushy. If they begin to dry out, add a little hot tap water. By the end of cooking, they should resemble a thick soup or stew.

In a sauté pan, heat the oil over medium heat. Add the onion and sauté for 2 to 3 minutes, or until translucent. Add the tomato, garlic, and chile and sauté for about 5 minutes, or until the tomato is fully cooked.

Transfer the tomato mixture to a blender and process until smooth. Add to the beans and stir in the cilantro and salt. Taste and adjust the seasoning. Serve warm.

To store the beans, let cool completely, then refrigerate in a lidded container for up to 5 days.

COOK'S NOTE: *You can freeze the beans and then add the tomato mixture, cilantro, and salt after you thaw them. Thaw the beans in the refrigerator overnight, and season them when you reheat them.*

ACKNOWLEDGMENTS

Mil gracias to the La Palapa family—all those who have helped us along the way from concept to creation, and from the time we opened our doors at La Palapa to the publication of this, our first cookbook. We would not have been able to do it without each and every one of you.

Special thanks to Domingo Torres, our chef and friend, whose patience and passion helped us develop many of the recipes included in this book; to Judy Maeda for her dedication to La Palapa; and to all of our restaurant staff—wonderful managers, great servers, hard-working cooks, prep cooks, and dishwashers—you make it all possible!

Special thanks also go to Diana Kennedy, Vicky Cowal, Barry Goodman, Andrew Klein, and Phil Scotti for their mentorship. *Muchas gracias también* to Kathleen Clement, Jennifer Clement, and Víctor Manuel Mendiola for carrying spices, mirrors, inspiration, and love up from Mexico in their suitcases.

Thanks also to these amazing people and organizations: François Chatelain, Eddy McGraw, Samareh Eskandaripour, Mark Hervey, Robert Hill, Martin-Jobes Design, Tamara Stack, Michael Palladino, Jimmy Adamic, Dr. Suzanne Mallouk, David Rainey, George and Lee Sibley, Gabriel Brezic, Alexandra Mitchell, Liza Al-Rajhi, Greg Callander and Ira Davidson of the SBDC, Ophira Edut, Valerie Stern, Jan Marklin, Eli Kopelman, Dominick, Mr. Solaris, Bob and Nick, Vivian Sorenson, and Ted Allen.

Our gratitude goes to Michael Bourret of Dystel & Goderich Literary Management Agency for his passion for La Palapa; he has been committed to our project at every step of the way. Mary Goodbody brought our authentic Mexican cuisine to life with skill and style; Lisa Thornton organized the recipes. Clancy Drake at Ten Speed Press provided excellent editorial oversight, vision, and guidance; Leslie Evans performed a thoughtful copyedit; and Sharon Silva added her extensive knowledge of Mexico to her editorial skills. The great photography team of Lucy Schaeffer, Heidi Johnson, Penelope Bouklas, and Shane Walsh grasped the concept immediately and had the ability to see the colorful beauty in our food.

Margaritte would like to thank her family and close friends for their loving support, patience, and understanding—I hope you know how much I appreciate all that you do so that I am able to do what I do!

Barbara would like to thank Sadik for inspiring the creation of La Palapa; Arielle and Alexander for their love of guacamole; and my family—you know how much I miss Mexico every day.

INDEX